Virtually Yours

Rebecca Newenham

Virtually Yours

Copyright © Rebecca Newenham 2020

ISBN 978-1-913713-14-0

Published by Compass-Publishing

Edited and designed by The Book Refinery Ltd
www.thebookrefinery.com

A catalogue copy of this book is available from the British Library.

Dedication

This book is dedicated to anyone who is at a crossroads in their career and unsure of where to go next, but sure that they want to work in a flexible and fulfilling way.

My family have been and remain a huge source of support to me in running Get Ahead Virtual Agency, and I'll be forever grateful for their faith in both me and my capabilities.

I also want to give a shout out to my business coach Nell, my friend Lara and my book coach Alexa, who have all kept me focused and encouraged me to make my dream of writing a book a reality!

Get Ahead wouldn't be the success it is without my amazing team and client base – you rock!

Foreword

Having spent 14 years in the franchise sector as a franchisor, franchisee, industry influencer and franchise growth specialist, I love the industry and what it offers to people.

Rebecca and I met in 2016 at the start of the Get Ahead Virtual Agency franchise launch. For me, it was a pleasure to see Rebecca's passion for getting her model right from the start. Refreshingly, this was putting people before profit to ensure that the early adopter franchisees had confidence in this proven model, ongoing support, launch packages and a business to suit their ideal work-life balance.

Many people miss the opportunity that UK franchising brings, as they don't take the time to explore what it can present to them. The Get Ahead model suits people looking for a second career, an opportunity to get a better work-life balance, and the chance to run a remote and scalable business; not many franchise models have this flexibility.

I tread carefully on which franchise models I endorse until I understand the franchisor's motivation; I'm very confident in endorsing Rebecca and her franchise model. Take a look and find out if it suits what you need.

Berkeley Harris – *Managing Director, Sandler Training.*

CONTENTS

Introduction

I'm the founder of virtual outsourcing agency Get Ahead Virtual Agency (Get Ahead). After the birth of my children, I found myself at a real crossroads, torn between wanting to spend time with my family and wanting to develop a fulfilling career. I've written this book for people who are in a similar position to where I was in 2010, dissatisfied with their current predicament and unsure of their purpose, but certain that there has to be more than the rigid nine-to-five working structure.

Get Ahead provides remote business and marketing services to our clients, who are busy business owners. Our clients love outsourcing to us, as it provides them with a flexible level of support, rather than the rigidity of employing people.

In this book, I'm introducing you to a way that you can be your own boss, run a Get Ahead office and follow our tried-and-tested model to develop a flexible business that fits into your life. This is your chance to have a second career to be proud of, rather than sacrificing your work for a flexible lifestyle. I want to highlight now that this book isn't right for someone who wants to work as a virtual assistant (VA) or for someone fresh out of university looking for a classic first career.

Recognising dissatisfaction

The fact that you've chosen to spend your precious time reading this book tells me immediately that you're open to change. I'm guessing that you've chosen to read this book because you're considering a more flexible way of working or you are simply interested to learn how you could possibly get that longed-for work-life balance! Perhaps you're feeling really stuck and finding it hard to see how you can have that dream life. Don't worry, before I set up my business, I felt just the way you feel right now. I used to hear people talking about their work and how rewarding they were finding it, and it felt like a foreign concept to me. Since starting to work for myself back in 2010, I have never had the dreaded Sunday-night feeling, and I love having a flexible work-life balance. You can have that too, and I'm going to show you how as this book unfolds. I wonder how open-minded you are? Have you been looking at various ways to work for yourself or is this your first time exploring this possibility?

A desire for alternatives

How would you feel if I told you about a solution where you could be your own boss, run a team and have a scalable business, whilst still receiving ongoing support and mentoring? You know you want more out of working, but you aren't sure what that is or what it looks like. The good news is that you're now ready to explore some alternative options for working flexibly without sacrificing the type of work that you do to achieve this. Often, we're led to believe that the only way you can work flexibly and within your own control is to do work that isn't as rewarding, or work that won't stretch and stimulate you. This book is here to prove that there is the opportunity to get interesting and scalable work in a way that will fit around your lifestyle. I have three teenage daughters, and I've always been determined to prove to them that I was available for them at the same time as making them proud of the work I do and the people that I help, as well as having time for myself and the others in my family. Just imagine how having a flexible business model could impact your life and put an end to the work-life juggle!

Understanding purpose

So, you know you want something more, but you're not sure what?

At some point in their lives, most people need to step back and reflect on their purpose. I think this happens at various stages of our working career. For me, it happened after having children. This felt like a natural time to review my career to date and see where I wanted to go next. It was a normal point to look ahead to see where I wanted to go with my life. Our working needs change over time, and we need to acknowledge this, embrace this opportunity and take the appropriate action. Our purpose can change over time too, so this a great moment for you to reflect and really engage with your own self-worth. Do you want to be your own boss? Do you want the opportunity to work part time? Does the thought of working from home inspire you? If it does, then this book will be a great way for you to understand how this can all be achieved as well as fulfilling your purpose in life.

How COVID-19 has changed the way we work

At the time of writing this book, we were hit by the COVID-19 pandemic, the prevailing lockdown had a *major* impact on how people worked and working from home was obviously a government order! As lockdown hit, I featured on a couple of local radio programmes, sharing my tips on how to work from home effectively, and how to work around your partner and children. Having worked in this way for the last 10 years, I certainly had a lot of tips to share!

Lockdown has allowed many people to assess their current working situation and see that working from home is possible (and we're seeing it being encouraged by people and employers who, in the past, wouldn't have given working from home any air time at all!).

This is a big opportunity for the VA industry, as people are pivoting their businesses. We've secured a number of new clients since lockdown because their businesses have moved online and they no longer need a presence in a physical office, and we're being described as the glue for their teams, which I love.

This is great news in terms of opening up a VA agency too. During lockdown, we've secured five new franchisees to run their own Get Ahead offices, which is super encouraging. There is a higher-than-ever demand for high quality VAs, so it will now be even more important to look at how you can use this to your advantage, and this book will hopefully show you how working from home can be so beneficial.

How to use this book

If you read this book in order and do the relevant quizzes, then I know you won't be disappointed. Something for you to think about as a reader is that there are two types of people in this world: those who read books like this and do nothing, and those who put what they've read into practice, take action and get immediate results. Reading is all very well and good, but to get the most out of this book, it's all in the doing! Enjoy.

 We've used our animated franchisee, Geri, to highlight important notes throughout this book using a branded Post-it note, so look out for these! Geri is a tongue-in-cheek version of me, and we have a cardboard cut-out of Geri who accompanies us to business exhibitions and is quite eye-catching!

Naturally, there is the use of some jargon throughout this book, and this is explained as we go through, but to help at this stage, here is a brief key:

» VA – Virtual assistant; a remote worker who provides admin and marketing support to clients

» Regional director – Our franchisee who runs a Get Ahead office for a defined geographical region in the UK and who manages a team of VAs to support their clients

» Client – Busy business owners who love outsourcing to us as they simply pay for the work that is done, and there are no other costs associated with this support

We also have a frequently-asked-questions (FAQs) section at the end of the book, which you'll find useful, and you can also look at our website for more clarification: www.getaheadva.com

At the end of each chapter, I've summarised the information into key takeaways, which makes it easy to remember the important facts.

I'm passionate about flexible working and providing amazing opportunities for people to be able to lead the life they deserve. Enjoy reading this book; take it at your own pace; do get in touch if you have any questions at all, however small; and if you feel you're my next franchisee, don't hesitate to get in touch...

CHAPTER 1

Purpose

"Some people dream of success, while other people get up every morning and make it happen." – Wayne Huizenga

"The meaning of life is to find your gift. The purpose of life is to give it away." – Pablo Picasso

---

In this chapter, we'll be talking about the importance of finding your purpose. By this, I mean really identifying what you want to get out of your working life. It's really easy for us to all fall into a career – perhaps one that we thought we ought to do or one that our parents suggested – and we don't always spend time being honest with ourselves and truly questioning if the work we're doing is really what we want and desire. Today, it's widely accepted that we can have multiple jobs and careers, and that our skills and interests can change over time, which is absolutely fine too! We can find that we naturally fall into a job, maybe have children, and then perhaps our original career isn't actually what we really want to be doing now. This certainly happened to me. It wasn't until I had a career break that I was able to spend the time researching business opportunities and acknowledge the fact that I was naturally drawn to being in charge and, ironically, that I wanted to be my own boss!

In this opening chapter, I'll be covering the following areas:

✓ Purpose – What this is and how we can find it

✓ Frustrations – Recognising and acknowledging those common work frustrations

✓ Compare and despair – How not to fall into this trap of constantly looking at others, comparing ourselves with them and assuming they have the perfect work-life balance!

Explaining recognition of purpose

Finding and acknowledging your purpose is essential in order to help you identify the type of work you would like to find. I really love the Japanese concept called *ikigai*. It's all about finding joy, fulfilment and balance in our daily lives, in both routine and in rituals. It's the reason for getting up in the morning! It's so easy to view our family, work, friends, passions and interests as separate entities when, in fact, they're so closely entwined. *Ikigai* views nothing to be separate; everything is connected.

This is certainly how I view my life. It's finding the balance and connections that are so vital. Once you achieve this, where and how you spend your time makes perfect sense.

Chris Myers 2018, founder of BodeTree says this:

> *"The fundamental truth of* ikigai *is that nothing is siloed. Everything is connected. This realisation has changed my outlook for the better. It is possible to be true to your passion, live a life of consequence, and still use business as a medium of expression."*

I feel that I've achieved a real sense of *ikigai,* but it has taken a while to get there! The following visual clearly demonstrates how you can achieve *ikigai* in your life by linking what you love, what the world needs, what you can be paid for and what you're good at. The sweet spot in the middle is your *ikigai.*

Take a look at the following *ikigai* visual, and then complete your own visual by writing words, ideas, pictures or sentences that relate to each heading:

Figure 1 – Ikigai Venn diagram. Source: Myers (2018)

» What you love

» What you are good at

» What the world needs

» What you can be are paid for

To help you do this, answer questions such as these:

» What makes you tick?

» What touches you?

» What are you good at?

» Which unique talents do you have and which can you develop further?

» What can you do that is of use to others?

» Is there something you can contribute to the world?

» What change would you like to bring about in the world?

Search for the overlap of the various circles; e.g. you may well be a natural communicator, so this could be an overlap between what you're good at and what you can do that is of use to others.

Spend time looking at the complete picture and try to find connections. Make sure you give ideas and impulses a chance, and keep an open mind. That way, your *ikigai* will eventually become clearer.

Please keep your *ikigai* safe, and we'll come back to this later (in Chapter 2).

It's also useful to spend some time thinking about how work can reward you in other ways apart from with monetary benefits.

 Take a look at this exercise from *What Colour Is Your Parachute?* (Bolles, 2019), and be honest with yourself. Rank your answers in order of importance too. Write your answers to the following question. This will really help you to identify your purpose for working, define what is important to you and, hopefully, will get you thinking more broadly.

Which non-monetary rewards would you like from working?

» Adventure

» Challenge

» Respect

» Influence

- » Popularity

- » Fame

- » Power

- » Intellectual stimulation from fellow workers

- » A chance to be creative

- » A chance to help others

- » A chance to exercise leadership

- » A chance to make decisions

- » A chance to use your expertise

- » Others

Once you have completed this exercise, you may be ready to start writing out your purpose, but if you aren't, don't worry.

Having a greater understanding of your own purpose will really help you to identify the type of work you're looking for – such as the opportunity to be flexible, to run a team or to be challenged; there are so many factors involved here, so it's worth spending time on this and not rushing the thought process. Spend time thinking about what *you* want to do – not what your partner wants you to do! Write these thoughts down; I always find it useful to carry a notebook with me and even have one by the bed for those 3am inspirational moments!

I'm hopeful that, after reading this book, you'll be looking at what we have to offer as a great solution to your career goals.

Frustration – why it's a motivational killer

I feel that we need to look at the reasons for frustration in our lives and how this can manifest itself. A lot of emphasis is put on the children myth. This states that, as soon as you have a family, your whole focus will be on your growing family, and work will slot into place and fade into the background. Well, hello, this isn't actually always the case! I know a number of women who have struggled with the dilemma of having kids but still wanting the career and all that it brings. I don't need to tell you about the cost of childcare, and the constant battle going on in your head between wanting to pursue your career and, at the same time, being around for the children you longed for. This is a continuous juggling act, and it can fill your head night and day. We're often led to believe that having a family is the ultimate reward and that we'll be fulfilled immediately, and how dare we wish for more? This juggling and feeling of constant frustration at not achieving anything properly can be such a motivation killer, and I talk to lots of women who assume that this is how it will always be, and that they should be happy with their lot and keep their true feelings under wraps.

We're led to be believe that having a family is the best gift a woman can be given, so we're naturally filled with guilt if we dare admit that being a mother isn't enough. It's actually only natural to crave a balance in our home life and work life. Why should we have to put up with a job that doesn't fulfil us, just because we have a family? This seems so unfair and super frustrating.

One of my team isn't a parent, but, interestingly, she felt slightly trapped within the corporate environment in that it had reached the point of no return. She was doing a good job, but she couldn't progress any further. She loved the work that she was doing, but it was the traditional format that she didn't enjoy anymore. She wanted to take control of her own destiny, to free herself and to be motivated.

So, have no fear – it's natural to still have a growing sense of frustration even if you feel you've ticked all the boxes by having children, but you also have a sense of needing more. This is totally normal, and don't feel alone or guilty for feeling this way.

What's important is finding a career that can allow you to enjoy *both* aspects of your role. Surely, having a job that gives you the flexibility and time to enjoy being a parent, whilst still challenging your 'working persona' is a win-win situation? I'll be going into this in more detail in Chapter 3, but, for now, I can assure you that you can have both.

Compare and despair

It's a common problem, but easily done, to compare ourselves to others and assume that everyone else has nailed their work-life balance. Just head over to Instagram or Facebook and spend five minutes there, and you can happily come away thinking that you're the only one doing the juggle! This comparison can be demoralising and can easily cause you to feel inadequate. But you need to remember that people rarely shout about their true feelings online and they are seldom honest in the playground. We're encouraged to show our best selves to the world at all times. I remember dragging myself out of the house on the school run when my third child was only days old, and a friend commented on my lipstick! Little did she know the effort and planning that had gone onto getting us all out of the house on time that day. However, I had clearly showed up with the appearance of having got everything under control, which wasn't actually the case! Looks can be deceiving, and we should all remember this, rather than jumping to conclusions. You need to be really wary about spending too much time on social media, especially if you're feeling in any way vulnerable; you can get swept up in it, and this can sometimes add to your feelings of inadequacy.

In the past, I often looked longingly at my contemporaries as they rushed off to get the train to London, glammed up in their work clothes, hastily kissing their children goodbye at the school gates and preparing for the run down the hill to jump on the commuter train. But isn't the nine-to-five corporate life glamorised? The pressure to make the commuter train, possibly standing for the whole journey. The stress of needing a work-clothes wardrobe, with the joy of office politics thrown into the mix. I truly believe that there is no glamour with this pressurised juggle either; it's more the case of the grass being greener on the other side. Spending time comparing yourself to others is a complete waste of time, and I really want you to stop doing it!

Also, we've seen a huge difference in how we *can* work with the COVID-19 pandemic of 2020. Working from home was actually a government order, so now, more than ever, working from home is the norm; hopefully, this will resonate with how you can really make a success of a home-based career.

The corporate nine-to-five isn't the solution

It's also easy to assume that the only way to make a successful career is in the traditional, corporate way. We've been led to believe that, once you have children, they have to fit into your lifestyle, and that nurseries and after-school clubs slot into place to support you and help you maintain your corporate life. However, I believe and know for a fact that you can you do credible and professional work in a much more flexible way that ticks all the boxes!

Supporting your working life with the use of childcare can be extremely expensive; you only have to watch the news to see women who say that, once they've paid out for nursery fees, they're virtually working for nothing. This can be extremely demotivating, and I understand why a lot of women look for alternatives to their original career once they're on maternity leave. There is a real myth that the only way to be taken seriously in your work is if you're wearing a power suit and hotfooting it into the city. This is absolute rubbish, and I'm going to be talking about this in much more detail in the next chapter and showing that the nine-to-five isn't the perfect solution that we're often led to believe it is.

KEY TAKEAWAYS

- **The importance of finding your purpose**
  This is achieved through really being honest with yourself and understanding what your motivators are for working, both monetary and non-monetary.

- **Exercise from *What Colour Is Your Parachute?***
  Do the exercise outlined in the first half of this chapter and keep the answers safe.

- **No comparisons**
  You need to recognise our natural ability to compare ourselves to others, and how damaging this can be to our self-esteem if nothing else.

- **Challenge the traditional**
  If there is one thing I want you to take away, it's to challenge the traditional ways of working, and to recognise that professional and credible work can be achieved in a non-traditional and much more flexible way.

- **Not everyone has it right**
  I want you to open your mind and realise that not everyone has it right.

- **There are alternatives to the nine-to-five**
  I want you to recognise that there are other ways of working than slogging your guts out in a tradition nine-to-five role, never seeing your children and never feeling good enough.

Case study – Rebecca Newenham

Before we move on to the next chapter, here is a case study on me and how I moved from being a stay-at-home mother to running my own flexible business.

Rebecca Newenham, founder and director of
award-winning Get Ahead Virtual Agency

I founded Get Ahead in 2010 after recognising there was a gap in the market for virtual-assistance services that offered the flexibility, value and performance that small businesses and start-ups need in the digital economy of the 21st century.

After a corporate career in buying for retail giants such as Superdrug and Sainsbury's, I was looking for a flexible work solution that could fit around my lifestyle and my three daughters – who are now 19, 16 and 14 at time of writing. Having grown up with a successfully self-employed mother, I knew it was possible to be able to contribute financially to the family, and to do school drop-offs and pick-ups too. My mum was a great example, and I grew up knowing that I wanted to run my own business one day, just like she did. Having looked at various business ideas and the way the employment landscape was shaping up for the future, I felt a virtual-assistance business offered the best solution. I've always loved networking, which is such a big part of my role now.

I now run a vibrant team of over 40 VAs and six regional directors, each bringing with them a particular skill set in many areas of business, including public relations (PR), marketing, social media, business development, account management, design and administration. Many of them are mothers themselves, and they also benefit from the flexibility that working for Get Ahead delivers. One of the team members – Jo Munroe, regional director for South Yorkshire – has said, "I love working for Get Ahead. No two days are ever the same!"

The business has won a variety of awards, including 'Flexible Business of the Year' in the Mum and Working Awards, and Theo Paphitis's 'Small Business Sunday #SBS Award'. It has also been shortlisted in awards for talent attraction and networking, and was selected as one of the best home businesses in the UK. I myself have been shortlisted for the Women in Business 'Woman Business Owner of the Year' award.

Why did you set up your own business?

I had a career break whilst my children were young, and I always knew I wanted to work, but that it needed to fit into family life too. I loved my career as a retail buyer, but I also realised that it would be hard to make this work effectively when the girls were young. Plus, I recognised that this was the perfect time to look at how I could work for myself and be in charge, but also have a team. I did a lot of research, always knowing that I wanted the work I did to be taken seriously and that it must be scalable too. I did a lot of work on myself, recognising my own purpose, and this led me into wanting to set up and run my own business that had a team.

What do you love about your business?

I love the fact that I'm making a difference to our clients' lives, but also making a difference to our team. There are so many skilled people out there who are struggling to get work that is fulfilling, rewarding and financially viable, as well as juggling children and lifestyle. Our clients benefit from our flexible and expert support, as and when they need it. I love that everyone is winning! I really enjoy business exhibitions, and we love meeting new people and engaging with a variety of other businesses. This is really refreshing, and you can learn so much from these events. Networking plays a large part in our work, and I always love making new connections.

What challenges have you had to face?

Like any small business owner, there have been many challenges along the way. Knowing when to invest and in what has been key. A few years ago, I made a major investment in a new website, which proved to be really worthwhile. It made a real difference to our reach online, and it helped to develop social media as a key referral channel for our business. I also made the decision early on that I wasn't going to work in the evening and at weekends. I needed to give my family this commitment, and it has meant that I've had to be highly efficient with my time management and to-do lists! I've also worked hard not to compare myself with others. I've always been clear on my business path and where I want to go. There is always competition around, and I've made sure that I see this as healthy, and I've made an effort to collaborate and share ideas within the VA industry, rather than seeing everything as a direct threat. We all know that people buy from people, and you have to have conviction in what you do and how you do it. A lot of time can be wasted comparing ourselves to others and spending too long hanging out on social media.

What are your future plans for the business?

I'm particularly excited about welcoming new franchises. We already have regional offices in place across Leeds, Berkshire, East Midlands,

South Yorkshire, The Wirral, Suffolk, Essex and Surrey. I really enjoy bringing new franchisees on board and supporting them to achieve their dream of running their own successful business. With the continued uncertainty over Brexit (and now COVID-19), we see more and more companies outsourcing to remain agile, which leaves VA businesses such as us and our franchisees perfectly placed to assist.

What advice would you give to other people thinking about starting their own business?

Don't be afraid to follow your dreams. Do your research up front and then just get on with it. If things don't turn out quite as you thought first time, don't panic – just think about how you could do it differently. Keep evolving until you get it right. Avoid comparing yourself to others and just enjoy the journey.

CHAPTER 2

The Problem with Nine-to-Five

I now want to demystify the idea that working in a traditional nine-to-five role is the only way to be seen to be doing a 'proper' job. In the past, if you weren't dressed in a power suit with a laptop bag, how could you possibly be doing a job that was worthwhile? To be seen as the real deal workwise, you needed to be commuting, always in a rush and heading for a tower block in the city.

Roll forwards five years, and you're no longer deemed an imposter if you work from a café, wear casual clothes and mainline coffee from the local Costa Coffee. I really want to delve deeper into why we always feel the need to follow the traditional route when considering how we work, and I hope that I can show you that professional, serious and meaningful jobs can be achieved in a non-traditional setting.

In this chapter, we're going to cover the following:

- ✓ Pressure
- ✓ Commuting
- ✓ Mindset
- ✓ Another way

Pressure

So why is it that, for women, as soon as their maternity leave is up, they immediately feel the pressure to go racing back into their old job or give up completely? It would appear that these are the only two options; or are they? Whilst it makes a lot of sense to go back to the job that you know, things have changed and a baby has come into your life, so this needs to be accommodated. There is a lot of pressure to do the nursery drop-off – or get a grandparent involved or find a child minder – and then go racing into work and crack on with your day.

I'm going to focus on mothers here for a moment, but this scenario isn't exclusive to them. I'll talk later (in Chapter 4) about a real-life scenario where two ladies who don't have children got to the stage in their careers where they had to find an alternative, as the traditional career path and nine-to-five just wasn't doing it for them anymore.

Throughout our lives, we have various career cycles, some come to a natural break (e.g. childbirth or children starting school) and others come out of the blue (e.g. as a result of redundancy). In the past, there has always been the assumption that we're all striving for the perfect job, and we can only be taken seriously if we're working long hours, day and night, we dress correctly, and we have no work-life balance. But who are these people that have made this assumption?

You only have to look at LinkedIn or Facebook to see how pressurised people are feeling in the workplace, due to all the demands of working core hours and racing back home at the end of the day. There is rarely a safe place to vent these frustrations for fear of being judged. I'm a member of a number of Facebook groups on flexible working, and they're full of women negotiating hard after returning from maternity leave, feeling really emotional anyway with the prospect of all they're leaving at home, only to struggle to get a decent part-time working package that won't take them out of the house for longer than necessary.

All these factors play a large part in helping you to realise and recognise that *working for yourself* is a far better all-round solution, and it doesn't mean that you're in any way less successful.

Letting go of the commute, for starters, plays a huge part in providing a more ideal working life, and letting go of assumed pressure to conform to the nine-to-five does even more so!

Also, let's look at the devastating effect COVID-19 had in the early part of 2020. Suddenly, we were commanded to work from home, and whilst a lot of office workers were able to do that, a lot became furloughed (urgh, I hate that word), and it took a lot of people by surprise.

The next section was written pre-COVID-19, and although a lot of businesses were able to go back to having staff working in offices after lockdown, the lure of working from home – now people have realised it actually isn't that bad – is more tempting than ever.

Commuting

Let's look at commuting for a moment. As discussed already, in order to fulfil a lot of 'proper' corporate jobs, commuting is necessary. But commuting can be hugely detrimental to our health and other factors of our well-being.

The Royal Society for Public Health (RSPH) (2016) released a study that highlights the impact of travelling to and from work by rail, bus and car on the public's health and well-being. It explains how commuting frames the workday, with the potential to set the tone of an individual's day at work, and therefore impacts their behaviour elsewhere.

The main points of this report are as follows:

- Longer commute times are associated with increased stress, higher blood pressure and body mass index (BMI), and a reduced amount of time available for health-promoting activities, such as cooking, exercising and sleeping.

- Commuters spend an average of 56 minutes travelling to work each day, with research indicating that this has increased in recent years.

- There is growing evidence of the detrimental impact of lengthy, non-active commutes on our health and well-being.

- Commuting can reduce mental well-being and negatively impact physical health.

- Inactivity poses a major challenge to the public's health.

These points prove immediately that commuting can have a really negative impact on us as individuals, not only at work but outside of it too. So why do we continue to feel that 'proper' jobs have to involve a commute?

In 2017, a study of more than 34,000 workers across all UK industries – which was developed by Vitality Health, the University of Cambridge, RAND Europe and Mercer – reviewed the impact of commuting on employee health and productivity, and these are its findings (Vitality Health, 2017):

- Individuals who commuted to work in under 30 minutes gained an additional seven days' worth of productive time each year, as opposed to those who commuted for an hour or more at a time.

- Longer commutes appear to have a negative impact on mental well-being, with 33% of workers with longer commutes being likely to suffer from depression.

- Of workers with a longer commute, 37% are likely to have financial worries.

- Of workers with a longer commute, 12% are likely to report multiple aspects of work-related stress.

- Of workers with a longer commute, 46% are likely to get less than the recommended seven hours of sleep each night.

- Of workers with a longer commute, 21% are likely to be obese.

These are quite shocking findings!

These studies all show how commuting every day can have a serious impact on us as individuals, and therefore challenges the view that commuting to work is the only way to be taken seriously in our employment. Surely, removing the commute would only have a positive impact on both health and well-being?

I really struggle when people assume that, just because you work from home or in a small office, the work you're doing is insignificant in some way. Who are these people that feel this way? And do you really care? The first step to realising that your journey is your journey is to let go of this judgement and understand that working in a different way can be just as valuable as working in an office.

It would appear that, over the years, we've allowed these beliefs to be taken seriously, which really is crazy when we're in a world where flexibility and virtual working is growing daily. In a recent Chartered Institute of Personnel and Development (CIPD) (2019) survey, it states that more than half of UK workers (54%) work flexibly in some way, and these statistics will only increase over the next few years. This has certainly been the case as a result of lockdown (March 2020).

People are starting to recognise that the cost of commuting can be really expensive too, so workers take-home pay is significantly dented by both this and the cost of childcare when appropriate. Job opportunities that eliminate commuting are certainly becoming more attractive, and businesses are recognising more and more that flexible working and working-from-home opportunities are hugely worthwhile. Imagine a job where you only have a 20-second commute; *how amazing would that be?* Keep reading to find out more about this opportunity.

Mindset

I really feel that the sooner we can all recognise that you can work professionally, in a job that makes a difference, without having to spend hours commuting or working in a traditional way, the better! Lockdown as a result of the COVID-19 pandemic has been drastic, but, ironically, it has shown that working from home is a viable option for almost anyone, whatever their role in a business.

It all really boils down to mindset, confidence and the ability to have a clear vision. Your vision enables you to get the best out of your situation in a realistic way. We covered *ikigai* in Chapter 1, and once you've identified your reason for getting up in the morning, this will help you formulate your working vision. Go and revisit this exercise. If you didn't complete it, have a go now and really try to nail down your purpose. Once you've got this firmly outlined, it makes the decision on where to go next so much easier. For me, I wanted a business for myself. I no longer wanted an unpredictable boss telling me what to do, and I wanted to rid myself of the dreaded Sunday-night feeling! It was so important to me to be working in a way that fitted with my core beliefs, but, at the same time, was doing something that was professional, was a business I could be proud of, and that had legs and could grow and evolve.

Another way

It's so important that the time you invest in your working life benefits *you*, and that you're getting the fulfilment and satisfaction that you deserve. Being your own boss is certainly a good contender for providing you with these benefits, but if this scares you and you think, *How on earth can I be my own boss?* then read on. This book will outline exactly how you can do that!

Self-employed people are the happiest workers in the UK, according to new research from a group made up of experts from the universities of Sheffield and Exeter, which surveyed 5,000 workers in the UK, US, New Zealand and Australia (Hall, 2018). The research concludes that, even though self-employed people have less job security and often no pensions, they remain happier and more engaged with their jobs than their employed counterparts. They really appreciate their greater freedom and independence.

If we've learnt anything from the COVID-19 pandemic, it's that having a job that is secure and able to withstand something as drastic as 'Stay home, save lives, protect the NHS', it's being able to have a job you can do at home.

Knowing that you have the tools, the mindset (Chapters 3 and 5) and the support (Chapter 6) will give you that opportunity.

If you think you're ready to have a chat about how you can join our team, get in touch (email us at office@getaheadva.com or call us on 01483 332220).

The mumpreneur myth

I need to mention the term 'mumpreneur', as no doubt you'll have come across it. I hate it! Why should I – a business owner who has children – be labelled as a mumpreneur? It feels as if I'm being pigeonholed and popped on a shelf, filed under that word. When I should really be seen as an entrepreneur and business owner who, if you delve deeper, happens to also have children. Yes, I'm doing the mum juggle, but this shouldn't be how I'm solely viewed. It's both patronising and demoralising in my view.

'Mumpreneur' is defined as "a woman who combines running a business enterprise with looking after her children" ('mumpreneur', n.d.). Whoop whoop – you have a child, you run your own business and you're now known as a mumpreneur! This is hardly a worthy title. As people often say, you don't hear the term 'dadpreneur', and if you did, no one would take is seriously.

It's good to recognise that the term exists – there are awards for it too – but it's a derogatory term in my opinion. By viewing mothers who work as mumpreneurs, it immediately raises the assumption that you can't ever be seen as truly professional as you have kids, you're a part-time mother and you're a part-time business owner; you'll always have to make sacrifices, and you're missing out on the responsibilities of a full-time mother! This is crazy, and I'm writing this book to show you that you can have children (or not) and still run your own professional business that is seen as the real deal by everyone!

It's fine to use the mumpreneur label to begin with, but be careful not to let it define you going forwards.

Virtually yours

Female business owners now account for one-third of business start-ups according to the Office for National Statistics (ONS) (2019), and, for the first time, more women than men (58%) are in self-employed roles. These women have followed a passion, but have also recognised that this style of work is so much more attractive, as it does fit around family and personal life.

- ✓ Flexibility around family care is the number-one reason for women with children to start a business (HM Treasury, 2019).

- ✓ Women are nearly five times more likely to mention family reasons for becoming self-employed than men. One-fifth of females choose to work as self-employed to help combine 'family commitments / wanted to work at home' and employment in a flexible manner (ONS, 2019; Prowess, n.d.).

 Imagine having this balance in your life, where you're seen as a professional business owner to the outside world, but, inside, you're also able to juggle your work life and find satisfaction in all these different areas. Imagine no longer having the dreaded Sunday-night feeling. Imagine sitting at your desk in your PJs just because you can! Imagine planning your day so all your meetings are carried out between 10am and 2pm, and your team is busy supporting your clients whilst you concentrate on your business development and networking? It really is possible to work professionally in this way and get real job satisfaction as a result.

So, the tide is turning, and – as the statistics have shown – there is a huge rise in the number of female business owners who are setting up successful and professional businesses, and there is no reason why you can't do the same. I appreciate that there is a lot to think about – confidence, mindset, work-life balance and mental health, to name just a few – and we'll be covering these in much more detail in the next chapter.

KEY TAKEAWAYS

- **Letting go of the commute-only route**
  We've shown that you don't need a commute to validate the professionalism of your work. It makes total sense to go to work without the time-consuming commute, as this will have a positive impact on your health and well-being too.

- **Don't let perceived judgement stop you from being your own boss**
  You might not have considered being your own boss in the past, but don't discount it now. There are so many reasons in favour of running you own business and being your own boss.

- **Positive impact**
  Research has identified that, even though self-employed people have less job security and often no pensions, they remain happier and more engaged with their jobs than their employee counterparts.

- **Being your own boss is simply better for your health**

CHAPTER 3

Being Your Own Boss

Having established that commuting and working the traditional nine-to-five isn't necessarily the right path for you, we're now going to look at what it takes to be your own boss. Just imagine being able to manage your own time and enjoy the freedom that comes with that! No longer reporting into someone and avoiding the dreaded Sunday-night feeling – heaven! Of course, there are pros and cons to being your own boss and running your own business, so let's delve into what it would feel like to be in charge and the attributes needed to achieve this sense of freedom.

In this chapter, we're going to cover the following:

- ✓ Self-employment statistics
- ✓ Being your own boss
- ✓ Work-life balance
- ✓ Mental health
- ✓ Key skills you need to develop

Self-employment statistics

Let's now look more closely as some of the more important statistics on self-employment in the UK.

The latest figures from the ONS (2019) indicate that 15% of all UK workers are now classified as self-employed. The UK is home to 5 million self-employed workers, and this figure are rising monthly.

A 2017 study (Gough, 2017) reveals that a typical self-employed worker makes £5,000 per annum (pa) more than the average national salary, despite working 10 hours a week less – fantastic news!

In January 2019, FreeAgent released a study of 1,000 working people in the UK, which looked at their reasons for being self-employed and their concerns. This makes for interesting reading.

Top three reasons to be self-employed (FreeAgent, 2019):

1. Better work-life balance (46%)

2. Wanting to choose the type of work they do (44%)

3. Attaining a greater sense of achievement (35%)

It's interesting to note the overriding importance of a better work-life balance; we'll be covering this in more detail in a moment. As a nation, I feel that we're, quite rightly, putting more emphasis on how we spend our time; why should we be a slave to tradition and always assume that we have to be working in a corporate role with a boss to be successful?

Top three concerns of being self-employed (FreeAgent, 2019):

1. Financial burden of setting up from scratch (34%)

2. Lack of government support for freelancers and small businesses (33%)

3. Managing company finances (31%)

I feel that these concerns are all ones that can be rectified easily with the right support, and they shouldn't put someone off setting up on their own. It's useful to acknowledge concern over finances, but with the right planning and guidance, this shouldn't hold you back. Our business model provides an extensive support network and knowledge base, so although our regional directors are running their own businesses, they benefit from ongoing mentoring and support in a safe environment. I know they really value this unconditional support, which means that they never feel isolated or alone, but they still know they're in charge and they benefit from this autonomy.

"The brilliant thing about becoming a Get Ahead regional director is that you start your own business, but you don't do it alone. Get Ahead offers all sorts of support to get you off to a flying start, so you'll have the freedom of being your own boss, alongside the security of an established brand. This was one of the overriding factors in helping me to decide to become a Get Ahead franchisee." – Jo Munroe, Regional Director, Get Ahead, Yorkshire

 Here are the top high-level positives of running your own business:

✓ Loving what you do

✓ Earning potential

✓ Work-life balance

✓ Flexibility

✓ Ability to choose your clients

✓ Control

Being your own boss

So, you want to be your own boss – here are some big reasons why the thought of this is so appealing:

- You can achieve an improved work-life balance.

- There's no office politics.

- You can control your own destiny.

- There's no need to explain your movements to anyone; you're the master of your own schedule.

- You can profit from your passion with increased motivation and morale.

- You're in a unique position to be able to design the life you want.

- You'll have flexible working hours and flexible location too.

- You'll get a greater sense of satisfaction, as you're in control.

- You'll have enhanced networking opportunities throughout the day and evening.

- You'll get a broad learning experience, as you're now human resources (HR), marketing and accounts.

- You can pick your own circle – or professional family, as I like to call it; you're in charge of who you work with in your team and also on the client side.

What you think a boss looks like   vs   What a boss can really look like

And now for the downsides of being your own boss:

- You'll have a heavier workload, which you'll need to manage effectively, but with the right help it will be relatively easy.

- You'll work long hours.

- It can be lonely.

- You'll still have responsibilities to uphold, and you'll be accountable to the people around you.

- You'll have to deal with all the hard conversations that you might otherwise have passed on to your own boss.

- It requires a full-blown mindset shift when working for yourself.

Having outlined some of these downsides, I promise I'll address these in Chapter 5 and explain how our training and ongoing support will combat all of these.

So, having outlined the pros and cons, I'm hoping you can see that there are huge advantages to running your own business, that you can see how attractive it is to manage your own time and workload, and that you can see how you can get great satisfaction and reward from being solely in charge. Having an entrepreneurial mindset allows you to benefit from the freedom, success and joy that managing your own business brings. Plus, you can learn and develop the skills that come with dealing with new areas of responsibility and new challenges. This is such an exciting time, and I really want you to embrace it all.

Work-life balance

Work-life balance is defined in Lexico.com (formerly Oxford English Dictionaries online) as "The division of one's time and focus between working and family or leisure activities" ('work-life balance', n.d.).

As noted in the FreeAgent (2019) study, achieving a better work-life balance is often at the top of people's to-do lists when reviewing their career, and so it should be! We have limited time, and we should be encouraged to get the balance right as often as we can.

Let's look at the impact having a better work-life balance can have on us:

✓ Health and well-being – By having more balance between working and relaxing, our health and sense of well-being can only improve. This will have a positive impact on how we feel about ourselves, others and our working life. It really is a win-win situation!

✓ Be more productive – With a better balance between work and the rest of our life, our productivity will only improve. We'll have more energy to do the work we need to do, we'll be more focused, and therefore we'll achieve more and be more productive.

✓ Actually enjoy work more – If we make time for ourselves through personal development, exercise, holidays, etc., we'll actually not resent the time we're working, as the balance will be much more aligned.

✓ Avoid the fear of missing out (FOMO) – FOMO is quite a buzz word at the moment! It's advisable not to let your personal life suffer by stressing over work. You need to train yourself to concentrate on what is right for you, and this will avoid worrying unnecessarily that you're missing out.

Combine this with the possibility of juggling childcare (as mentioned in the last chapter) and having a much less stressful commute, and you can see why this option is so attractive.

Case study – Marie Peters

Areas of expertise: Digital media, marketing and business operations

Here are 60 seconds with our regional director Marie, who joined the business after a 15-year career in London, juggling family life too, and you can see why she loves being part of Get Ahead and running her own office:

When and why did you join Get Ahead?

I joined in January 2020. I had been looking for a bit of a change in direction after spending 15+ years in the same industry (and commuting to London!), when – by chance – I met the Get Ahead team at the Women in Business Expo in Farnborough. The proposition and opportunity really stood out to me, and things fell into place from there!

What did you do before you joined Get Ahead?

I've worked for global media agencies for all of my career. I started out doing media planning and buying for a wide variety of large clients, and from there I moved into operations-focused management roles.

What is your career highlight to date?

I really enjoyed my time in the media industry; it's fast-paced and ever-changing, and there were many highlights. However, I would have to say taking the plunge into running my own business with Get Ahead is the most exciting thing I've done to date! I love the autonomy, combined with the support from Rebecca and my fellow franchisees. I'm able to plan my own time and meet such a variety of people. No one week is the same – I love it!

What are your plans for the future?

I'm loving meeting and connecting with businesses in Surrey, building relationships and learning new skills as I go. It's an exciting time to join the Get Ahead team as it grows and expands into new areas – both geographically and in terms of the services we can offer. I love having more quality time with my family, and I'm not missing my major commute one bit!

It's clear that a better work-life balance has such a positive effect, and these benefits can be far-reaching and affect more than just yourself. As Marie mentioned, she's certainly not missing her daily commute into London! In our fast-moving world, we really need to take the whole work-life-balance scenario seriously, and not treat it as some woo-woo fad! This leads us on nicely to talk about mental health, which is a very hot topic at the moment and one that we all need to have on our radar.

Mental health

The pressure of an increasingly demanding work culture in the UK is one of the biggest challenges facing our mental health. Mental health includes our emotional, psychological and social well-being. It affects how we think, feel and act. It also helps determine how we handle stress, relate to others and make choices.

In the UK, one in six people experience mental health problems in any given week. A key way to protect your mental health against the potential detrimental effects of work-related stress is to ensure a healthy work-life balance. To get this balance, you need to work smarter, not longer. You need to work at drawing a line between work and leisure, avoiding a long commute, and taking decent breaks at lunchtime, for example. It's important to recognise the importance of exercise, leisure activities and friendships too. As the old saying goes: healthy body, healthy mind. It isn't productive to overdo things, and you need to look after and protect your own mental health. The beauty of working for yourself means that you can look after yourself; you can have a 'duvet day' if necessary, as you're in charge. This is so liberating and shouldn't be undervalued. You're the boss, you're in charge and you really need to maximise on what this actually means for your well-being and confidence too.

 We do need to mention COVID-19 again here (are you getting sick of this yet?), but it has taught us some really interesting lessons. Above all, we've learnt a lot about ourselves and how we operate.

Those of us who thought of themselves as an extrovert, actually are more of a closeted introvert, and vice versa. Shifting from a possible commute or office environment to working from home may well have impacted you in ways that you weren't expecting. So, it's important to talk often, exercise and have a genuine support network to help you avoid any possible feelings of isolation.

Owning a Get Ahead franchise provides you with the support that you need, and getting a good work-life balance is at the forefront of this opportunity. It's why the business was set up, and the franchise model allows you to manage your time and achieve this longed for balance. It's a reality not a dream. Get in touch if you want to learn more about how you can do this (email office@getaheadva.com or call 01483 332220).

Key skills to develop for becoming your own boss

We're now going to look at a few key personality traits that we can assign to being useful when you're your own boss. If there are a few things on the list that scare you or put you off, don't panic, as we'll run through our opportunity in more detail in Chapter 4, which will reassure you!

So, let's go through a few common traits and skills that are needed if you're to succeed at being your own boss (these will be discussed in more detail in Chapter 5):

Mindset

Having a boss-like mindset means that, when you're faced with challenges, you'll have the strength to see them through. Your consistent approach to running your own business, managing a team and winning clients' all need you to be positive, clear and open. Having the right mindset and showing up daily with this same attitude will be critical to your success.

Passion

Being passionate is a useful trait as this means that you'll take your work seriously, you'll want to make it a success, and you believe in what you're doing and why you're doing it. Having passion and conviction are infectious, and this will come through in all that you do; it will empower those around you to believe in what you're doing too.

Flexibility

Having a flexible approach when running your own business will help you to appreciate and understand that you'll need to be involved in quite a few activities at the start. Having a flexible approach will help you to be more open-minded and understand what is involved in running your own business.

Keenness to learn

It's essential that, as your own boss, you're keen to learn and develop, self-motivated and a good listener. It's important that you're comfortable being the decision-maker.

Relationship builder

You need to have a natural interest in people, be keen to develop and nurture relationships, and be curious. I love learning about people, what makes them tick, what they're doing and why they're doing what they're doing. Being in business is all about relationships and communication, so this trait is one of the most important for me. Running your own business means you need to be comfortable attending events, for example, and be confident in your delivery when speaking to others.

Vision

Having vision means you're aware of the need to set goals and be clear about how you want your business to look. This doesn't mean you have to do it alone, but you do need to be able to look ahead and visualise how you want your business to be.

Entrepreneurial spirit

A boss needs to have a touch of entrepreneurial spirit about them! A need to be creative, and being opportunistic, proactive and visionary are all good traits of someone who is their own boss.

Discipline

You need to have any element of discipline in your working day, so you can get the best work-life balance. Being constant and consistent are essential, and you always need to show up, or you need to make a conscious decision not to show up, understand why this is and be comfortable with your decision. This is such a big topic that I've expanded on this in Chapter 5.

Time management

If you can nail your time management, everything else will fall into place. I find using a to-do list is my number-one activity to help me get focused and make the most out of my day. At the end of the week, I review my week ahead and write my to-do list, and there is nothing more satisfying than crossing tasks off as I go. I've even been known to add a task to my list that I've already completed just for the satisfaction of crossing it off again!

Identifying opportunities

As the boss, it's essential that you always have work opportunities on your radar. You need to be able to recognise an opportunity and then use your imagination and initiative to nurture and grow it into a credible piece of work. This plays into the need to always be aware of your marketplace and be thinking creatively.

So, having looked at what you'll need to cultivate, fill in the following word-cloud box with some of your *key* traits that you think will help with this. For instance, if you're good at time keeping, list that. If you're organised and love a to-do list, then that is most definitely a positive.

Word-cloud exercise

Word-cloud example

Use the two blank word clouds – on the opposite page – to fill in your positives (the first one) and concerns (the second one). You can use the following words for inspiration or come up with anything you feel fits either word cloud.

- Structured
- Disciplined
- Responsible
- Motivated
- Versatile
- Flexible

- Passionate
- Confident
- Consistent
- Honest
- Trustworthy
- Efficient

Word-cloud positives

Word-cloud concerns

As you can see from these tips, there is no right or wrong way to run your home office. There will always be a sense of trial and error, but I hope I've shown you that, with a clear daily plan, you can be super efficient, your own boss and still have a productive work life. (In Chapters 4 and 6, we'll be looking at this in much more detail.)

KEY TAKEAWAYS

It's totally normal to have concerns when you're thinking about running your own business. At the start, it can feel daunting, you may be worried about feeling alone and isolated, you might miss having someone to share ideas and concerns with, and you might wonder if your business will be a success. Panic not! Our solution in Chapter 4 resolves all these concerns.

With clear planning, discipline and focus, you can be super productive at running your own business from home, and benefit hugely from an amazing work-life balance.

- **Work-life balance**
  A better work-life balance has a positive impact, not only on your health and well-being but on your productivity and self-worth too. It's amazing how much more fulfilled you can be once you have the balance right between your work and your personal life. Once this is in sync, everything else falls into place.

- **Mental health**
  Mental health is a real buzz word at the moment; however, it has been recognised as being an important factor because many of us tend to spend the majority of our time at work. A key way to protect your mental health against the potential detrimental effects of work-related stress is to ensure a healthy work-life balance.

- **Key traits of being your own boss**
  We've covered a number of key personality traits that help when you are your own boss, and our top five have to be these:

  » Entrepreneurial spirit

  » Passion

  » Vision

  » Mindset

  » Relationship builder

CHAPTER 4

The Alternative Solution

In this chapter, I'm going to introduce you to an alternative solution – an amazing opportunity that will give you the flexibility you're craving, and a way to run a business that is professional, scalable and, ultimately, super rewarding. However, if you aren't interested in growing a team, working from home and organising your own time, then this probably isn't for you!

In this chapter, we're going to cover the following:

- ✓ The 'what now?' quiz
- ✓ Different types of businesses you can set up
- ✓ The business model that is the best of both worlds
- ✓ Demystifying the myths of franchising
- ✓ Our business model
- ✓ The benefits of working with us
- ✓ A case study on one of our franchisees

To kick-start things, I would like you to take this quiz and answer all the questions truthfully (www.getaheadva.com/what-now-quiz), and I'll happily give personal feedback.

The 'what now?' quiz

1. Have you had a full-time career?   Yes/No

2. Are you working at present?   Yes/No

3. Are you working full time or part time?   Full/Part

4. Are you on a career break? If yes, for how long?   Yes/No
   (If yes, then is returning to your old job off putting? Why?)

---

5. Are you feeling bored or overwhelmed about your career?   Yes/No

6. Are you concerned that you're too old for a career change?   Yes/No

7. Do you feel something is missing from your current working life?   Yes/No
   (If yes, then what is missing?)

---

8. Would you like a new career that is home-based and flexible?   Yes/No

9. How much time do you have available in the week?   hrs

10. Would you be happy managing and growing a team?   Yes/No
    (If yes, does this excite you? If no, would you be willing to learn?)   Yes/No

---

11. What income are you looking to earn?   £_____

12. Do you own a car or are you able to travel?   Yes/No

13. Have you worked from home before?   Yes/No

14. Has your career background included any of the following areas (please tick each that applies)?

    Sales / Marketing / HR / Office management / Other (please list)

---

15. Would you be comfortable networking and talking in public?   Yes/No

16. Have you ever run your own business?   Yes/No

17. Do you like coffee?   Yes/No

18. Do you have money to invest in your career?   Yes/No

19. What excites you from this list?
    Being your own boss / Working from home / Freedom / Running a team / Managing your own time / Meeting new connections / Flexibility

The different types of business you can set up

Hopefully, by running through the quiz, you're now getting really excited about the thought of not only working flexibly and at home, but also that you could be running a business that ticks all the boxes, including being a business that you can be proud of! You may well have thought in the past that the only way you could possibly have a flexible work-life balance would mean sacrificing the work that you do. I've seen so many friends confess apologetically to taking a teaching-assistant role at a school because this was all that they could think of doing to give them the flexibility that they needed. There are women at my local primary school who have had mega jobs in the city before having kids, and who are now on playground duty because they wanted to be there for their children after school. Schools are benefiting hugely from this highly skilled resource, but I know that this isn't the only solution for someone who is craving flexibility. My team are truly proud of being business owners. They hold their heads up high at dinner parties when people ask them what they do for a living; gone are the apologies, and in their place are the smiles of pride because my team are living the dream: they're in charge of a growing business that is satisfying not only their clients but their own team too. It's a win-win situation all round.

Which one is best?

One of the first decisions you need to make when setting up a business is to decide what type of business to set up: sole trader or limited company. Let me explain a bit about each option, and then you can see what is on offer.

» **Sole trader**

A sole trader is when you're in business on your own and you don't set up a limited company at Companies House to run your business through. When you're a sole trader, you're self-employed, and – legally speaking – you and your business are one and the same.

You register with HMRC so that they know about your new business, and they expect a tax return from you every year.

» **Limited company**

A limited company is where the company is a separate legal entity from you. You'll most likely be a director of the company (you run it) and also a shareholder in the company (which means you own all or part of it). This is a more costly way of running the business, as you'll pay more tax, but you have protection as you and the business are two separate entities.

Being a business owner sounds great, but there are some pretty shocking statistics on how many small businesses fail in the first few years. According to the ONS (2018), the one-year business survival rate in 2018 was an average of 89% and the five-year survival rate was only 42.4% on average. There is always concern over cash flow, finding clients, getting paid, etc. – the list goes on. From the outset, you have to manage everything from deciding on a business name, designing a logo, building a website, working out who your customers are, determining where you need to go to find them, attending networking meetings and organising your marketing; basically, you start off being everything from graphic designer to PR manager to accountant, with all these roles as well as the pressure of earning money! Of course, you always have the option of engaging someone else to do some of these tasks for you if you have the budget to do so!

They both sound pretty demanding, don't they? However, there is another way: in this chapter, I'm going to explain our business model, and you'll hopefully see that it's a winning combination of being your own boss, yet having a safety net.

Going solo

Ordinarily, setting up your own business can be quite daunting. You can expect to feel a rollercoaster of emotions, but we're going to show you how these feelings are resolved by being part of our franchise – the Get Ahead family.

Loneliness

Setting up a new business and being in charge of everything yourself has the potential to be daunting and isolating. If you've come from a corporate job where you sat in a large office with all the mod cons, then working from home suddenly with only the radio for company could be a shock! However, we'll cover top tips on working from home in Chapter 5, and, actually, you aren't alone, as you'll have access to the other franchisees and team members. As you'll see from the case study later in this chapter and the day in the life of a franchisee, your week will involve a number of networking meetings and opportunities to meet others. I promise that you'll really value the peace and quiet that will feature throughout your week!

Poor self-discipline

Having self-discipline is needed when running your own business, and if you are starting out from scratch, this can be pretty exhausting. The beauty of our franchise model means that we know exactly what is involved from the outset, so you're given full training, and you'll have a clear plan of what is expected of you and your business. Although the business isn't competitive, it helps that there are other people running different regions, so you can share best practice and get sensible tips on helping you keep on track. Our monthly team call is a great opportunity to chat and learn from each other too.

Stress

It's inevitable that you could be concerned with dealing with the stress of setting up your business. There's a lot to think about – the competition, growing your client base, team issues, making money, etc. – but you aren't alone with Get Ahead. The model is tried and tested, and you can get support on anything you're concerned about, so this feeling of stress should be minimalised.

No time off

There is always an anxiety about how you can never have a break from your business if it's yours! You often hear horror stories of business owners who haven't had a holiday for 10 years since setting up their business. I've always made sure that I have proper breaks throughout the year; this is why I set up my own business, surely? I encourage all the franchisees to put holidays in place, and we can cover emails and phone calls centrally. It's critical that we all experience the benefit of taking time off from the business and not letting it rule our lives. The business model allows for client work to continue, with or without you!

Financial concerns

Without a tried-and-tested model, it would be hard to know when you might expect to make money. With our franchise, we have a clear financial model that plainly shows how you can scale the business and the areas to focus on. This is super helpful and reassuring.

The business model that's the best of both worlds

My business – Get Ahead – is a virtual agency. 'Virtual' means that our work is carried out remotely – from home, actually! We've divided the country into regions, and each one is run by a director who manages a team of VAs who carry out the work for our clients. My team of directors (possibly including you) all work from home – in some cases, from their kitchen tables!

Our business opportunity is actually set up as a franchise. Our regional directors are franchisees who buy a five-year licence from us, which allows them to run a Get Ahead regional office for us. They're their own boss, but they have our constant backing, support and training. This is such a fantastic way for you to run a tried-and-tested business for yourself and to be part of something bigger.

Demystifying the myths of franchising

At this stage, I feel it's important to touch upon the term 'franchise' and what this really means, as I know it can be associated with greedy franchisors, hefty fees and little in return!

The franchising model explained

Franchising is defined as follows (Asefesco, 2015):

> "A continuing relationship in which a franchisor provides a licensed privilege to the franchisee to do business and offers assistance in organising, training, merchandising, marketing and managing in return for a monetary consideration. Franchising is a form of business by which the owner (franchisor) of a product, service or method obtains distribution through affiliated dealers (franchisees)."

If buying an existing business doesn't sound right for you, but starting from scratch sounds a bit intimidating, owning a franchise could be the perfect solution.

So, just what is a franchise? And how do you know if you're cut out to be a franchisee?

A franchisee pays an initial fee and ongoing monthly royalties to a franchisor (10% of turnover each month in our case). In return for this investment, the franchisee gains the use of a trademark, ongoing support from the franchisor, and the right to use the franchisor's system of doing business and sell its services.

Buying a franchise offers many other advantages that aren't available to the entrepreneur starting a business from scratch. Perhaps the most significant is that you get a proven system of operation, and training in how to use it. New franchisees can avoid a lot of the mistakes start-ups typically make, because the franchisor has already perfected daily operations through trial and error.

Franchising has grown significantly in the UK and is now worth £15 billion pa. A report by the British Franchise Association (BFA) (2018) identified that there were 44,200 franchisee-owned businesses in the UK employing 620,000 at that time. People are attracted to buying a franchise because of the autonomy and flexibility of being their own boss, but with the added support of the franchisor. It feels like a more secure way to run your own business than starting from scratch.

Examples of some well-known franchises are Spar, Costa Coffee, KFC, Kumon Maths and Molly Maid. All these businesses are run as separate franchises, but you get the same experience in each franchise. For example, a Costa Coffee in Guildford would look and feel the same as a Costa Coffee in Leeds. There is consistency in the training of the staff and in the products they sell. Each franchise follows the same training manual, which gives the customer the same experience, and this is the sign of a franchise working really well.

There are naturally a few downsides to running and buying a franchise that you need to be aware of, as follows:

- » Buying a franchise means you're entering into a formal agreement with your franchisor.

- » Franchise agreements dictate how you run the business, so there isn't a huge opportunity to be creative without prior agreement with the franchisor.

- » Restrictions apply regarding where you can operate your business and the services you can provide.

- » Buying a franchise means sharing a percentage of your monthly turnover on a regular basis.

Our model

Our franchisees thrive because they have the benefits of being part of an established, award-winning and profitable brand. We've been there, seen it and done it all before! As I've already mentioned, we have monthly calls, and this is a safe place for our team to chat things through and to ask for advice in a non-competitive environment. I'm always on hand to chat to my franchisees and support them however they need, whether attending an event with them or offering a spare pair of hands at an exhibition.

I've seen many business owners who feel out on a limb because they have no one to turn to for advice. Running a business shouldn't be lonely, but so many fail from mistakes that could have been rectified with the right advice and team around them. I'm passionate about sharing with and supporting my team, and this is reflected in our business model.

"With Get Ahead, you get plenty of support, including training and mentorship, and the knowledge that you're part of a bigger, national team. If you're thinking of opening a Get Ahead regional office, we say go for it!" – Suzanne Cox, Regional Director, Get Ahead, Berkshire

How it works

We provide our clients (busy business owners) with a variety of administration and marketing support. We find the best VA for the job from our wide pool of VAs.

Let's look at an example of one of our clients who needs support:

Jon is a classic example of our ideal client. He's a financial consultant with speaking gigs all over the world. Jon needs specific support in his business, but not on a full-time basis. He loves working with our agency as we're able to provide him with the exact support that he needs, as and when he needs it. Over the last eight years, we've designed Jon a new logo and business cards, made him a new website, answered his business calls, proofread his last two books, collated his expenses every quarter and even found someone to mend his laptop! Jon understands the true value of our support, he knows that we'll find the best people for the job, and he simply pays for the work that is carried out, with no hidden charges – simples!

In essence, a new client comes to us with their requirements (e.g. for a virtual personal assistant [PA] with social media experience), and we match them to the most appropriate member of our team, both on skill set and personality. Both these aspects are critical for making a successful match.

So, who are our clients? Well, we work with business owners of all shapes and sizes – the common denominator being that they're all keen to grow and to do this in the most efficient way possible. They love the fact that we can provide them with the appropriate level of expertise, as and when they need it. Our clients recognise the cost involved in employing staff – the payroll, insurance, sick pay, etc. – so we're a really appealing staffing alternative. Our clients often come to us because they need to stop doing all the roles in their business, otherwise their growth will be impacted. We can help them to let go of certain tasks, and instead concentrate on doing the things that they do best, and let us get on with the rest!

However, a big misconception about what we do is that you, the franchisee, become the VA. You don't. You become the director who handles the VAs and matches them to the clients.

This remote and flexible style of working is actually becoming more popular, even in larger organisations. There seems to have been a real shift in trust over the last few years – and even more so since COVID-19 – and almost every business has been forced to operate remotely. I set Get Ahead up in 2010, and some people just couldn't get their heads around how this level of support could work without the client and VA physically meeting up. Today, technology is such that sharing documents, speaking online, etc. is so easy that people are much more accepting of this way of working, and it's becoming more popular. With lockdown, 'Zoom' has become a household term that almost everyone is familiar with, and few people are scared of participating on a video call these days.

Because we provide a wide range of services to our clients, we describe the business as an agency. By 'services' I mean that we provide our clients with anything from a dedicated virtual PA or someone to answer our client's telephones via our call centre, right through to running their business's social media and providing PR specialists to promote them.

Our team members absolutely love working remotely, as it fits in perfectly with their lifestyle. Around 80% of our current team have children and really value the opportunity to work from home, combined with doing work that they love without a commute of any sort. They can even do a dog walk or walk the kids to school and still be back at their desk in time. A number of our team work in the evenings once the kids are in bed; anything goes, and this is why it ticks all the work-life-balance boxes.

Another key bonus of being part of our agency is the opportunity to be part of our community, the Get Ahead family. We have a closed group on Facebook, for example, so the team use this to share best practice, ask questions, or even enjoy a water-cooler moment and share jokes or funny memes. They all really value this resource and opportunity, which they couldn't easily replicate if they were working solely for themselves.

Why being virtually yours (with us) is so cool

I'm now going to talk about why being your own boss and running one of our franchises is so super cool!

You'll be part of an established business

As I've mentioned earlier in this book, I started Get Ahead in 2010, so we're certainly well established, both in Surrey (where I'm based) and now further afield around the country. This is so exciting and rewarding, and by buying a Get Ahead franchise you too could benefit from this recognition.

Our franchise model is quick and straightforward to set up. Our induction process is so thorough that you'll walk away with a clear guide of how to get going straight away. There is something so exciting about being part of a growing and expanding business. The energy levels are high, and we all feed off each other. It may sound cringy, but we really are growing our Get Ahead family!

The business model works; it's tried and tested, and is being tweaked all the time. As new franchisees come on board, we get a renewed perspective from them and we learn from each other. It's so stimulating, and I feel that we're never standing still, which is extremely refreshing too.

Your business will be scalable

One of the main advantages to running a Get Ahead franchise is that you build a team that will support your clients. Through networking and promoting the business, you're able to explain how you can support clients and help them with their business. Clients are able to really benefit from our agency model. You're able to explain about the breadth of services we provide, and our clients love that they can find all the solutions to their needs under one roof. They see you as their business dating agency! No job is too small, and as I've mentioned before, the team is never-ending as people are always keen to work for us as they love the flexibility that we provide.

Our model is exciting since there is no cap on your earnings, as you simply bring more VAs onboard to match demand. If you were working solely on your own, there would come a point when you would have to limit your client numbers, which would be seriously frustrating. This isn't the case for us, which is hugely motivating.

You can grow at your own pace

Our franchisees love that, although they're part of our wider team, they're still their own boss and can grow as much as they like within their territory.

As a regional director, you're in total control of where you network and who you work with. This is really liberating because you have us as a safety net at the same time. We're always here to offer advice and to simply be a sounding board, as we can no doubt answer any questions you have as we'll already have come across it! This is a huge positive, and it's this support that energises our team and keeps them motivated.

You'll receive ongoing PR and marketing support

Now marketing and PR are a huge minefield, as there are so many options and most of them involve spending money! This can be quite a challenge to a new business just starting out. This is why having a franchise with us is so beneficial, as you'll be backed up and supported by our national marketing campaigns.

You'll benefit automatically from our existing brand equity and strong social media presence. We have over 17,000 followers on social media at time of writing, and this can only rub off on your franchise from the start. We provide all our franchisees with a launch package in which we write a press release about you and send this out to all the local press, and this always has great results.

You'll have your own dedicated page on our website, which you can use to direct people to when you meet them at networking meetings and in your marketing. Our website has strong search-engine optimisation (SEO), and it means you don't have to invest in your own costly website. Our team page on the website is worth a look, as this is a really popular page, which proves that people love looking at our wider team and all the different skills we have under one roof.

Our first-class training and mentoring is a huge bonus to a new franchisee. We have a two-day induction course, and I love watching our franchisees gain confidence over this time as we share our proven techniques for running your own business. It's such a motivating and exciting time.

Our extensive training programme covers every aspect of running a successful Get Ahead franchise. Our team love the detailed and easy-to-follow manuals, which are simple to use and a great point of reference as your business develops. We're always adding to them too.

I set up Get Ahead as I witnessed first-hand the like-minded career women in the playground, who had amazing skills that weren't being utilised due to their inability to find work that fitted in with their childcare. I really wanted a chance to maximise this talent pool and to provide these women with interesting work without sacrificing their home life. Consequently, I've achieved just this, which is so empowering.

Although the team work remotely, they still love the chance to meet up face to face, and so do I! Pre-COVID-19, we had brunch to celebrate our business birthday and we met up in London for afternoon tea! The team travelled from far and wide, and I so loved hearing them chatting, swapping stories and laughing together. They all appreciated the chance to meet up, but, equally, they were unanimous in their passion for working from home and not in an office. They all said how much more efficient and less distracted they were.

Basically, you join our franchise by becoming a regional director, and you manage your own pool of VAs to support your clients' needs. The diagram on page 73 shows clearly how this works. However, you always have access to our core team of VAs, so there is no rush to build up your own team – phew! This is a huge advantage, as it takes away any pressure, and you can start supporting clients straight away. Imagine if you were starting this business on your own from scratch and a client asked you for some support you couldn't offer? That could be really tricky. However, with our model, you always know that we can find you the best person for the job. This is a huge advantage and you'll avoid any sleepless nights worrying about who can do the job.

OK, so we've talked about what our business does: we're an outsourcing agency. Our regional directors (franchisees) run their own branch (region) of Get Ahead. The region is built up of specific postcodes, centred on where the franchisee lives. We use sophisticated mapping software that plots postcodes and shows distinctly how many potential clients (small businesses) are based in each postcode. Having your own region makes it much easier to manage; you'll know where to go to market and what you do, and we can direct potential clients to the right branch too. Simples!

The next big question is where do the clients come from?

As I mentioned earlier, the clients are busy business owners who need support, but they can't justify employing people all the time. The cost of employment goes beyond just the hourly rate: you have to factor in holiday pay, sickness cover, tax and national insurance too. So working with us on a flexible basis is a no brainer.

Our clients come to us in a variety of ways:

- ✓ Through referral or personal introduction (we love this!)
- ✓ From a direct enquiry through our website (perfect!)
- ✓ From networking meetings (we love these too!)
- ✓ Through social media (gives us a big smile!)
- ✓ Email marketing (yay!)
- ✓ Exhibitions (one of our favourite pastimes!)

 Our opportunity is the perfect solution for someone who is looking for an exciting career where they can be their own boss and enjoy the flexibility of a good work-life balance, but not have to start from scratch and make all the mistakes first! We're here to support you with new clients from the start. We can review their requirements and help you match them to the perfect VA in our team. As time goes on, you'll do this yourself naturally, but it's really helpful to have our guidance in the beginning.

The picture over the page explains the different roles within the franchisee model. I go into more detail about this in Chapter 6 – *How to Make It Successful*, but, hopefully, you can see what part you could be playing in this model. You are the potential regional director/franchisee.

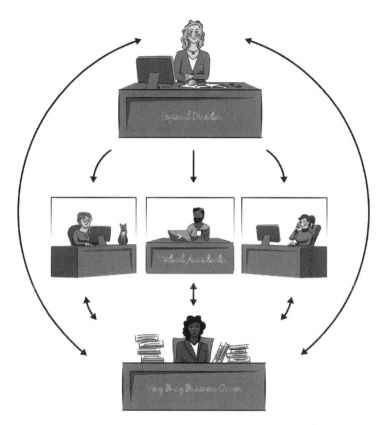

Who's who: regional director / franchisee (top); VAs / team member (middle); busy business owner / clients (bottom)

Importantly, franchisees enjoy the benefit of strength in numbers. The Get Ahead franchisees are non-competitive and super supportive. They all really value each other's opinions, and they love our monthly calls where we share best practice and support each other.

How to get clients

Referrals or introductions

We've been in business since 2010, so we're well established and people recognise us. Naturally, we get introduced to potential clients by existing clients who love what we do, from people we know in our area, and even from ex-clients who no longer need our support. Referrals are super special, and we really value these, as the prospect generally already knows a little about what we do before we even speak to them, and the sales process is then even more straightforward.

Direct enquiries

Every franchised office has a dedicated page on our website, and there is also an enquiry form on the website, which people can complete if they're interested in our services. We'll then direct the enquiry to the right branch.

Networking meetings

It's essential for a regional director to feel comfortable and confident enough to attend a networking meeting and be able to talk about our business to other people. I'm not expecting a top-class acting job here! I just need our franchisees to be professional and keen to meet new people. Obviously, the last thing I want is a regional director who doesn't listen to anyone and talks about themselves constantly; there's a fine balance to be struck. I see these networking meetings as an essential part of a regional director's week, where they will meet like-minded business owners, learn new things and, hopefully, meet some potential clients too. We provide our regional directors with full training on how to get the most out of networking, including what to say and how to say it! At the time of writing, we're coming out of lockdown, so all our networking is online and, consequently, our franchisees have been honing their skills at presenting via video instead of in person. It's amazing how much more concentration is needed when networking online, as you miss the non-verbal cues, but at least it's a way to maintain contact, and develop and nurture relationships.

Social media

As a business, we have over 17,000 followers across our social media platforms at time of writing, and our regional directors benefit from this activity as soon as they launch. We're constantly sharing relevant articles and showcasing case studies that demonstrate our expertise in flexible working. LinkedIn is a personal favourite of mine, and I love engaging daily with a wide variety of people on there. Our clients are active on social media too, so it's important for us as a business to have a strong profile. We provide bespoke social media training for every new franchisee as they join the business, which gives them the confidence to hit the ground running once they launch.

Email marketing

Sending regular emails out to our database is an effective way to educate our potential clients. We provide our regional directors with monthly newsletters, which are sent out to their own regional list. It's amazing how effective these emails are at reminding people of our existence and about our wide range of services. Our regional directors love them too, as we send them out on their behalf; they just give us their contact list, and it's job done! This is another huge benefit of working for us as a franchisee, as opposed to having to do everything themselves.

Exhibitions or trade shows

These are an effective way to promote our services and help find new clients too. There are normally annual business expos in every city, and, naturally, these attract busy business owners needing help. I encourage every franchisee to exhibit once a year, and we'll help give some money towards the exhibition cost. We've just exhibited at our first online exhibition, which was a totally unique experience, but one that will no doubt be repeated until face-to-face exhibitions happen again.

PR

Finally, when our regional directors launch with us in a new area, we invest time in writing a bespoke press release, and this is sent to local newspapers, online resources and websites. We always get positive results, as everyone likes an upbeat news story! The press release will give information on our new franchisee, and it will explain more about our business and the people we support. It is a great way to spread the word about outsourcing and how we help local businesses grow. PR is a fantastic way to introduce us to potential new clients, and we always thank publications for picking up our news stories, which helps nurture local links within the business community too.

So, I hope you're now clearer on our exciting franchise opportunity, in terms of what is needed to be a Get Ahead regional director, managing a team and supporting busy business owners who need specific help to grow their businesses.

What makes a perfect franchisee

We've looked at what the franchise side of the business looks like, so now I think it makes sense to look at our 'perfect' franchisee and what traits they have. These aren't set in stone, but will give you a clearer idea and, hopefully, you'll see yourself in these qualities! (I also go into more detail about mindset in Chapter 5.)

The main qualities we look for in a Get Ahead franchisee are the following:

- ✓ Someone with a background in marketing, HR, project management, sales or business development – Someone who is comfortable with our business, and who can see the benefits to the client, to the team and to themselves too.

- ✓ Good networker – Someone who is inherently interested in people, enjoys meeting new people, relishes in asking engaging questions and loves helping clients find the right solution for them.

- ✓ Excellent face-to-face business-to-business (B2B) skills – Our franchisees need to be competent in talking to others and representing us. Active-listening skills, for example, are key here.

- ✓ Experience in managing a team – As we've described earlier, the regional director's role centres around running a team and giving clear instructions. This won't suit everyone.

- ✓ Driven and ambitious – As a regional director, you're running your own business, and you need to have the fire in your belly to make it work.

✓   Entrepreneurial spirit – We aren't looking for true entrepreneurs who want to bring something totally unique to the business, but what we do want is someone with the spirit and energy of an entrepreneur. We've done all the hard work in setting up the business and proving it works, but it's your spirit that will enable you to make your mark on your own region and give it a unique personality.

Benefits of working with us (at minimal risk to you)

Starting any business requires a level financial outlay, and with this comes risk. Remember the shocking statistic of new small businesses and their rate of closure (page 60)? Well, with something like our business model, that risk is radically reduced, as you're buying into a proven method. We've tested it in so many ways, and we know how it works and what you need to do to get it right. We share our financial model as part of our early discussions with potential franchisees, and financial forecasting forms part of the franchisee's induction once they launch with us.

There are clearly many reasons why we're the perfect solution for you! I've summarised the main ones as follows, and the case study of one of our franchisees later in this chapter will hopefully bring it alive for you too.

Proven, scalable business model

We've been piloting the franchise model since 2017, so we know it works. The unique element is that the business is totally scalable. You'll always be able to find VAs to support your clients, so there is truly room to grow and develop your region, so your earning potential is huge. This is really exciting.

Home-based and flexible

Our franchise opportunity ticks all the boxes when it comes to running a business from home and giving you the flexibility that you crave and deserve. Gone is the two-hour commute and wasted time. With us, you can run a credible business from home and still offer a professional service to your team and clients; it's a real win-win situation.

✓ Low cost and low working-capital requirement – The only costs involved in setting up with us is the franchise fee. You're given everything else you need to set up and start marketing your business. You simply need a laptop and a good broadband connection, and you're off!

✓ No VA experience is required – This can be a misconception. We offer VA services, but I don't need our regional directors to feel the need to carry out any client work. We want people to run their region, and spend time networking and spreading the word, not doing the client work. Your virtual team supports your clients on a daily basis.

✓ No need to recruit employees – This is a massive bonus. From day one, you can start supporting clients by using members of our wider team. You'll always find someone with the right skills, so you won't need to turn any work away. If you were starting up from scratch, finding the team to work with could be a huge mission. We take this stress away from you completely.

✓ Provision of mentoring, ongoing training and support – When you set up a business on your own, it can be isolating, especially if you come straight from a corporate job with support on tap. Being part of our franchise means that you're never alone. You'll have mentoring and guidance from the very beginning, and this never stops. We're passionate about supporting all our team, and providing guidance and best practice. Our franchisees love that there is always access to training, both internally and externally. We're one big happy family! We want everyone to thrive and get the success they deserve, so our franchisees are non-competitive and extremely nurturing.

Now we've covered the main benefits of running a Get Ahead franchise. Perhaps you're still not sure about what our franchise can offer you? The following is a case study of one of our recruits who set up her franchise in Leeds.

Case study – Fiona Ibbetson

Fiona had worked for the head office of a retailer for a number of years, and she was a senior manager who was balancing her career with her family. She always felt that there would be a better work-life balance if she was managing her own business, but she was never really sure what she wanted to do. We met at a business exhibition in Birmingham, and it was a match made in heaven! Fiona felt that she was missing out constantly due to working long hours, and she'd had enough. Her children were growing up, and she felt that they needed her even more, particularly as her eldest child was about to start secondary school. Fiona was exhausted and felt as if she wasn't achieving anything or getting anything right, so something had to change.

This is what she said when I asked her some questions:

Why did you join the Get Ahead franchise?

I joined Get Ahead in January 2018. I had always wanted to run my own business, and – after researching a number of options that would utilise my skills – I met Rebecca. The business and the team are a perfect match for me, as they deliver real results for the businesses they work with, offering a flexible approach that suits the clients. The flexibility for me to work from home and still be able to do the school run is really valuable.

What did you do before you joined Get Ahead?

I worked for over 20 years in both retail and manufacturing. During this time, I was fortunate enough to have a diverse range of jobs, including being a project manager delivering software improvements to the business. I loved the pace and the people, but I decided I wanted to do something of my own.

What is your career highlight to date?

Meeting the Get Ahead team and completing my training, as this was the real start of my journey. Everyone was very welcoming and extremely helpful in sharing their knowledge in their areas of expertise. I know I'll have many more highlights in the coming years, with the support of the Get Ahead team to achieve them!

What is your typical working day like?

My morning routine

I like to get up early because I have a great morning routine that helps to get me in the right mindset for the day: half an hour of exercise, followed by ten minutes of daily gratitude. Then it's time to get the kids up and ready for school. I usually eat breakfast at around 8am and then check my emails to get an idea of the jobs I'll need to tackle first.

At my desk

The first thing I do when I sit down to start work is check over the tasks for that day that I planned for myself the day before: responding to emails, posting and engaging on social media, and connecting with people I met at networking events.

After that, I call the Get Ahead team to get a client update – it's always reassuring to know that I have that support there when I need it – and I follow up with clients to ensure that they're getting everything they need. This is also a good time to make contact with prospective clients.

Out and about

The beauty of being a regional director is that you aren't bound to your desk all day, every day. A big part of the job is networking, and I tend to do most of my networking at lunchtimes, in order to fit it within school hours.

If I'm not networking, I'll use this time to review my business and marketing plan, think about what is working well for me, and hone my pitch for future networking events. I'll take about half an hour for lunch and eat it at the table (not at my desk!).

Afternoon commitments

When my daughter gets home from school, I take a break to catch up with her, and then I walk to my son's school to pick him up. This isn't the end of the working day for me, but it's great that I can be around when my kids finish school, to ask them how their day was.

My afternoon jobs include checking my emails and social media again, and responding to anything pressing, such as sending a client proposal. As the working day comes to an end, I review what I've done, and plan my tasks and set goals for the next day. Then, at around 5pm, it's time to stop work and take the kids to tae kwon do!

Being a regional director for Get Ahead is a hugely rewarding job, and I love the flexibility of the working hours and the variety of every day. I would recommend it to anyone who's thinking of taking the plunge.

It's clear from Fiona's case study and day in the life that she's embracing life as a business owner and has found the true value in running her own office with the back-up of our national team. She's really engaged with every aspect of the business from day one, and she has found networking to be a real driver in helping promote her business to businesses in the local area. Fiona's confidence has soared, and she even hosts a couple of networking events too.

A quick word on what this isn't (becoming a VA)

At this point, I want to highlight what this opportunity is not! As you'll have seen from Fiona's profile, our franchisees are running their own office of our business. They're in charge of meeting new clients and matching each client with the perfect member of their team who will carry out the work. This is a business dating agency!

Our franchisees need to be active listeners, to be interested in meeting new prospects and to help them identify the assistance they need. As we all know, the clues about what people are really thinking or needing are often in their non-verbal communication. Our franchisees need to use their intuition, pick up on these signals and use this information in helping to match their clients with the right experts.

Remember, our franchisees *don't do the client work*; rather, they facilitate it by helping our clients find the perfect expert within our team who will carry out the work. This will then allow the client to get on with what they do best, which often gives the client back the time they need to grow their own business. Why should a client whose hourly rate could be £100 per hour spend hours doing admin that they could outsource to one of your team for £30 per hour?

So, we've established that you want to work for yourself, but the idea of setting up from scratch is just too much. There are so many options, numerous risks involved and a lot of uncertainty. I hope that, in this chapter, we've helped you see how powerful buying the right franchise can be for kick-starting your journey as a business owner in your own right.

KEY TAKEAWAYS

We've looked at the benefits of being a Get Ahead franchisee: being home-based and flexible; low start-up costs; the ability to scale it quickly; and ongoing mentoring and support. Hopefully, the case study on our franchisee Fiona has helped bring this opportunity to life, and you can easily see what a fantastic opportunity this is for you to become a Get Ahead regional director. You too can be your own boss, work flexibly from home with a growing team, and support some amazing clients on their business journey too.

- **Setting up a business can be risky.**
- **Getting the right business for you is key.**
- **Franchises are fab! They have so many ongoing benefits.**
- **Being a Get Ahead franchisee isn't being a VA.**

CHAPTER 5

Shifting Mindset

In this chapter, we're going to look at the importance of mindset and its impact on our working life. A positive mindset must be accompanied by a desire for discipline, and we're going to review some tips on how to keep on track and really benefit from running your own business. We'll then delve slightly deeper and see what a typical day looks like for a Get Ahead regional director, and we'll review the options of running this solo or in a partnership Exciting!

In this chapter, we're going to cover the following:

- ✓ Reasons for mastering a positive mindset
- ✓ Formulating a winning perspective
- ✓ Cultivating a positive mindset, from *Attitude is Everything* (Keller, 2012)
- ✓ The need for discipline
- ✓ A day in the life of a regional director

Why mastering a positive mindset is important

In order to achieve a better work-life balance, it's crucial that we review our mindset.

A person's mindset is their way of thinking and their opinions. If you refer to someone's mindset, you mean their general attitudes and the way they typically think about things. To be a successful boss and to run your own business, you need to demonstrate a positive outlook, and this needs to be projected in all that you do.

Running a winning company successfully takes an enormous amount of self-belief and tenacity, both of which are fuelled by how you feel about yourself. If you doubt your abilities or are always looking at the negative side of things, then when things do go wrong, catastrophic thinking could take over. Being able to adapt to high-pressure situations, thinking quickly on your feet when things don't quite go to plan, or turning a perceived negative outcome into a positive one will really help you get through those days where you want to hide away.

Being able to shift your thinking – or just being aware that you are in control of how you shape your day – will stand you in good stead when starting out. Reading more about this subject is something I would recommend, and there is a list of recommended reading at the back of this book.

Fixed vs growth mindset

It's worth understanding the difference between a 'fixed' mindset and a 'growth' mindset.

It's a little bit like nature vs nurture:

» People in a *fixed* mindset believe you're either able or unable to do something, based on your inherent nature, because it's just who you are.

» People in a *growth* mindset believe anyone can be good at anything, because your abilities are entirely due to your actions.

The fixed mindset is the most common and the most harmful, so it's worth understanding and considering how it's affecting you. For example, in a *fixed* mindset, you believe things such as, "She's a natural public speaker" or "I'm just no good at speaking in public". In a *growth* mindset, you believe, "Anyone can be good at anything. Skill comes only from practise."

In a *fixed* mindset, you want to hide your flaws, so you're not judged or deemed a failure. In a *growth* mindset, your flaws are just something you need to improve.

In a *fixed* mindset, you stick with what you know to keep up your confidence. In a *growth* mindset, you keep up your confidence by always pushing into the unfamiliar, to make sure you're always learning.

This all links in to what we looked at earlier about finding your purpose: in a *fixed* mindset you look inside yourself to find your true passion and purpose, but in a *growth* mindset you commit to mastering valuable skills, recognising that your passion and purpose come from doing great work, which in turn comes from your expertise and experience.

To be the most effective boss, and to be able to really motivate yourself and your team, it's advised that you work on your growth mindset.

Carol Dweck's book *Mindset: The New Psychology of Success: How we can learn to fulfill our potential* (2007) explains this beautifully here:

> "In a growth mindset, people believe that their most basic abilities can be developed through dedication and hard work—brains and talent are just the starting point. This view creates a love of learning and a resilience that is essential for great accomplishment. Virtually all great people have had these qualities."

Having a growth mindset is important as it helps you unleash your potential. I particularly love this description from the late author Henry Stanley Haskins: "What lies behind us and what lies before us are tiny matters compared to what lies within us." Our mindset shapes what lies behind us, before us and within us, so it's critical that it's positive and forward-thinking.

Having outlined the benefits of the work-life balance and introduced the idea that you can be your own boss, it's just as important to focus on your goals, your health and your positivity. You're your own cheerleader. What you think about consistently has a direct impact on your behaviour, so it's very important to believe in yourself and to understand the power of your mindset.

How mastering a positive mindset will help you:

- ✓ It develops a healthy self-esteem – People with healthy self-esteem feel confident in their own opinions, interests and beliefs. They're capable of making their own decisions, regardless of what everyone else is doing.

- ✓ It will help formulate a winning mindset – A winner's mindset keeps you focused and acknowledges that, whatever obstacles get in your way, you'll be successful in the end.

- ✓ It will help to harness drive – It's by using your drive that helps you make the jump into being your own boss. Drive, determination and passion are a winning combination for helping you make changes for the best.

Developing healthy self-esteem

Developing a healthy self-esteem in your franchise is important because – although self-esteem won't fix all your issues or help you sail smoothly through, struggle free – it will help you find the courage to try new things, build the resilience to bounce back from any issues, and make you more susceptible to success. However, it *is* something we have to continually work on and grow. Self-esteem levels at the extreme high and low ends of the spectrum can be harmful, so, ideally, it's best to strike a balance somewhere in the middle. A realistic-yet-positive view of yourself is generally considered the ideal.

Nathaniel Branden covers the value in developing a healthy self-esteem in his *Six Pillars of Self-esteem* (1995), and understanding these practices will help you navigate life and your business with a positive attitude, and will help you believe that you can accomplish your goals. I love the way Branden describes these different practices in a really relatable manner:

The practice of living consciously

So, live in the moment more! By expanding your consciousness, you'll also expand the world in which you live, because if you're aware of more, you can experience more. This, in turn, allows you to grow and develop. Try to direct your energies where they're really needed. When you live consciously, you channel your time and energies into planning and creating what you want in life, and you stop investing them in useless worries and negative internal talk. It's more productive to focus on the one thing that you can do in this very instance that will bring you closer to the result you want, rather than spending time worrying.

Putting it into practice

I've really worked hard at this, and it has proved really helpful in running my business. It's worth trying to stop knee-jerk reactions to everything that comes your way; for example, not reacting to an email the minute it arrives in your inbox. Instead, pay close attention to your thoughts and the emotions that accompany them, and then question their authenticity. Appreciate life more. You'll laugh at yourself and life in general, because you won't see life through a judgemental pair of eyes anymore. This is powerful and true!

The practice of self-acceptance

It's useful to work on improving what you can change and learning to accept what you can't. We can waste a lot of energy trying to alter things. Self-acceptance means that you understand who you truly are, and where your strengths and weaknesses lie. You know what you want. This will allow you to be comfortable with your place in the world and be honest with yourself. So be kind to yourself; accept that you might be a worrier and not enjoy turning up to meetings without preparing yourself fully.

Putting this into practice

Avoid worrying by preparing thoroughly before a meeting, practise your pitch and then you'll feel comfortable that you know all the facts. Confront your fears. I used to really dislike public speaking, and it all stemmed from a bad experience at school. I knew that I needed to work on this, so I invested in some public-speaking training, which really helped me to overcome my fear, and I soon realised that it wasn't as scary as I'd made it feel in my head. I also accepted imperfection and recognised that good is good enough. There will always be people who I see as better than me, who present all the time, so I just needed to let go of the ideal, accept myself for who I am and recognise my unique skills.

The practice of self-responsibility

This means having the strength to make the right choice when faced with a challenge. This is how you take control of your life, get in the driving seat and become more accountable. So, there's no blaming or complaining. Blaming others puts you in the position of playing the victim, and complaining is just another way to shake off responsibility. Together, they prevent you from making real changes. Don't take things personally; I've had to work hard at this as I've naturally blamed myself for things in the past. Remember, disagreements aren't personal attacks. Try to see things objectively and rationally, instead of reacting on impulse. There's great power in being able to make conscious, calculated choices.

Putting this into practice

Always keep your goals in mind, and choose your actions accordingly. I love the fact that all my franchisees bring a wealth of different knowledge and experience to the business. They're all managing their own regions, and I've observed that the ones who develop and grow the fastest are the ones who are constantly looking at how they can develop and who think out of the box. Successful people see a problem, analyse it and then come up with possible solutions. Writing lists and being disciplined are great ways to achieve control too.

The practice of self-assertiveness

This relates to being authentic in all that you do, having the confidence to believe in yourself and your actions, and being 100% unapologetic. Obviously, this comes with practice, but – as your own boss – you need to develop these skills so that you feel comfortable with your decisions at all times. This isn't about being pushy at all. Good areas to practise here are realising that changes are needed, believing in your rights, and figuring out appropriate ways to assert yourself in situations that concern you. Practising giving assertive responses and building your confidence by trying to be assertive in real-life scenarios is helpful.

Putting this into practice

Examples of practising self-assertiveness as a franchisee would be in communicating your needs clearly by feeding back to me, as your franchisor, what help you needed or changes you would like to see happen within the business. By not taking rejection personally, you're demonstrating your ability to be assertive. For example, if you did a client pitch but didn't win the business, you can practise self-assertiveness through your reaction, by understanding the need to not take this decision to heart, and by being able to learn something from the experience and move on. Remember that assertiveness can also be expressed with your body language: giving direct eye contact in meetings, and expressing your thoughts and emotions freely. All these techniques help reinforce a positive mindset and view on life and your business.

The practice of living with purpose

If you do something with purpose, it means you do it intentionally. Practising living purposefully means that you – as an entrepreneur and as your own boss – have a strong sense of purpose in all that you do. You'll pay attention to what brings you joy. As for me, I get my energy from face-to-face interactions, when I connect a new client with the perfect member of my team. Taking time out and making time for stillness and reflection really helps. In our busy lives, this takes practice.

Putting this into practice

I've recently found time for peace and reflection in walks with our puppy and in my Pilates classes. It's also important to be brave and come out of your comfort zone from time to time. Speaking opportunities have allowed me to do this. You also need to take action, as many of us live with limiting beliefs that we've had since childhood. Now is the time to let go of conditioned thought patterns and be open to new opportunities – such as running a franchise!

The practice of personal integrity

The very word 'personal' means what you believe in yourself; this is your very own unique frame of reference. Personal integrity means having a personal value system, and your behaviour – in your work and homelife – being in line with that value system. Branden (1995) doesn't see self-esteem or personal integrity as separate traits. They're traits that you continually practise and improve. You do this by building a harmonious personal value system and by behaving in a way that reflects your value system. This requires good old self-discipline and courage! Running a Get Ahead franchise and being your own boss requires you to be honest and to keep your promises to both your team and clients. Honesty is one of the most important aspects of integrity.

Putting this into practice

For example, when you're dealing with a new client you must always to truthful about what support you and your team can give. Whenever we introduce a new client to a member of our team, we always say to the team member that they must be truthful about whether they feel they have the right skills for the job. The last thing we want is for someone to pretend that they can help, only to then find that they've never used a particular system and the support doesn't work; this reflects badly on us in turn. To practise personal integrity, you have to show compassion and empathy towards others; this is super important when running a team. Our franchisees have a duty of care to their clients, their team and the wider group of Get Ahead franchisees. I always expect them to be understanding and kind, and to help others whenever possible. We're a team, and we need team players. As you practise personal integrity and the other five pillars, your self-esteem will improve, and so will your satisfaction from your work and life as a whole.

Formulating a winning perspective

A winner's mindset keeps you focused and acknowledges that, whatever obstacles get in your way, you'll be successful in the end.

Success is extensively based on our perspective and how we view the world. Whether we view things with a positive or negative slant can make all the difference. I'm naturally a glass-half-full person, and I'm attracted to people with the same positive attitude as me. Mindset has everything to do with perspective, and having an optimistic mindset increases our ability to form a winning perspective and therefore achieve longer-term success in all that we do.

When running your franchise, you'll attend a lot of networking meetings. Imagine you've driven a long way to visit a new meeting, and when you turn up, there are only five people there! Rather than see this as a negative, switch your focus and be pleased that, as there are only five people there, you'll be able to have meaningful conversations with them all.

A winning perspective helps you to see opportunities in all situations. Life isn't what happens to you, but how you choose to respond to it. You can either let your challenges work for you, or they become a barrier. That choice is down to you. Do you give up after multiple failures and rejections, or do you readjust your sails and carry on? A winning perspective will, of course, do the latter.

Motivational coach Kory Minor (2020) describes four areas for achieving a winning perspective, and I've adapted these for our franchise model as follows:

1. **Winning mindset** – Training yourself to have positive thoughts and, like me, trying to see the glass as half full. Having the strength to persevere. Being part of our franchise really helps with this, and we work a lot with the franchisees on planning their month's activities and going about their tasks with a positive attitude, reflecting on their day, learning from their experiences and planning ahead. Our monthly calls with the whole franchise team help embed this winning mindset, and the franchisees feed off each other's energy too. It's highly collaborative.

2. **Winning attitude** – Surround yourself with positive people, have a positive attitude and believe in what you're doing. Our franchise model is perfect for supporting a winning attitude. We have a specific WhatsApp group for the franchise and a closed Facebook group, so the team members share wins, best practice and questions; the team are all positive and upbeat in their support for each other. This really helps maintain a winning attitude across the whole team, which is super helpful.

3. **Winning focus** – Be clear about what you want to achieve and make happen in your day. It's important to be present to make this possible. You must be in tune with what is important to you. I love this quotation from Kevin Kelley, "Winners focus on winning. Losers focus on others." It's so much more effective to focus on what it takes to win and succeed than to always focus on what other people are doing. As part of the franchise, we set key performance indicators (KPIs)[1] and draw up an individual plan for each region, which really helps each individual franchisee to focus on what they need to achieve, to give them a winning focus and to give them the steps they need to achieve success.

---

1. *"A quantifiable measure used to evaluate the success of an organisation, employee, etc. in meeting objectives for performance"('key performance indicator', n.d.).*

4. **Winning determination** – If you aren't determined to win, then *what's the point?* You need to show up every day with the best version of you. This attitude is helped and supported by having a clear goal and vision. I've found that creating my own vision board is really helpful in giving me a clear idea of where I want to be, both in my work and my personal life. I've realised over the years that when you know exactly what you want to accomplish, you have determination. Often, people will come across an obstacle and see this as a reason to give up. Successful people see obstacles as a reason to keep on trying, and this is what we do within our franchise. If we come across any issues, we talk them through and come up with a solution. Our franchisees all demonstrate a winning determination, but this is also backed up and supported by me and the team. Of course, we'll always come up against unfair situations or treatment, but the keys are how we respond to these situations and having the determination to try again.

Our Bristol team is a great example of formulating a winning perspective. Alison and Claire are running their franchise as a partnership. Neither of them had experience of being their own boss; they both came from a corporate background in office management and were craving the independence of running their own business. Alison in particular was fed up with the Sunday-night feeling of dreading going back to the office on a Monday. We spent a lot of time in their induction looking at how they could harness a winning perspective, especially as they were working closely together. Neither of them had ever needed to sell themselves, so the thought of networking and selling not only themselves but their business services was really quite daunting. We recognised that they would need help with this, so – as part of their induction – they had bespoke training on speaking in public, and their confidence has really grown with practice. They're now confident enough to network independently too, which is great, and being able to cover double the networking opportunities is an advantage of running the franchise as a partnership.

They both struggled with explaining the value of the services they provide to their local community, most of whom always seemed caught up on how much the services would cost and overlooked the immediate benefits of the support we offer. This was tough for Alison and Clare, and this could have affected their business success without them having a clear focus and determination. However, with the support from the wider team, and with the benefit of a well-defined vision and plan of what they needed to achieve and how to achieve it, the Bristol team demonstrated consistent determination and a winning mindset; they are really growing their business now, which is great to see.

Harnessing drive

Generally, people with drive and ambition are focused and self-motivated, which are good traits of a positive mindset, and they also tend to strive to accomplish more; these are all great attributes for a boss! As a business owner running your franchise, it's important to be clear about what you need to achieve each week. Write a clear plan that includes a mix of activities that you can carry out from your home office (e.g. writing social media posts, and booking in 1-2-1s with networking connections), and activities where you'll be out and about (e.g. networking meetings and face-to-face meetings with prospective clients). In all your interactions, keep focused on your desired outcomes, be efficient in using your time and keep motivated. My mum has always said, "keep your eye on the prize" – I love this saying, and it really helps to keep me focused and on track. Give it a go!

Cultivating a positive attitude

Having looked at the fixed vs growth mindsets, why self-esteem is important, formulating a winning perspective and how to harness drive, let's now take a look at attitude.

Mindset and attitude are very closely linked: mindset determines attitude. Mindset is a collection of your thoughts, opinions and beliefs, which further shape your attitude towards a particular thing or a person. Remember that your attitude can be faked, because it's more of an external thing, but mindset determines who you actually are. If you have a positive mindset, it will help you achieve greater things. Mindset gives you goals, and attitude provides you with the ability to achieve these goals.

Jeff Keller, author of *Attitude is Everything* (2012), gives these tips on how to cultivate a positive attitude. I can relate to them all, but I especially like tip number three!

For each tip, we've shown how you can put these into practice:

Remember that *you* control your attitude

It's crucial that you recognise the power of your thoughts and actions. We can do the things we need to do when we need to do them; we have this choice. Some days, it's harder than others, but, ultimately, you can control your attitude and actions.

Putting this into practice

Wake up, say your positive affirmation and avoid looking at your phone until you're ready to start your working day. Don't let other things control your thoughts or attitude. Ideally, you'll write a detailed to-do list the night before, so when you're ready to kick-start your day, you'll simply have to review your list and get cracking.

Adopt beliefs that frame events in a positive way

It's possible to look at situations and find the positive in them. Initially, we may find we look instinctively at the negative in a situation when, actually, there will generally always be a positive to find or something to learn from a situation; we need to try to train ourselves to think this way. We need to be creative and find a positive explanation for something that happens instead of reverting to the habitual negative narrative.

Putting this into practice

A client may turn around suddenly and say that they no longer want to work with your team. You could see this as negative immediately; however, you could turn it around by refocusing on marketing your services at a new networking event and – because you're so clear on the type of clients you want to attract – you meet your ideal client immediately and sign them up straight away.

Create a library of positive thoughts

It's super powerful if you can concentrate and focus on positive thoughts and actions, rather than dwelling on negative ones. If you keep tuned in to what is working well, then you'll naturally enhance your energy, motivation and creativity. It's a win-win situation, surely!

Putting this into practice

You may well be anxious about attending a new networking event and think of lots of reasons not to go. However, if you research the meeting beforehand and understand who is going to be there, you'll be much more focused; plus, you can ask the person running the meeting to introduce you to a specific person who you feel could be your ideal client, and you can make sure that you get something positive from the event from the start.

Avoid angry or negative media

We're all aware of the impact of negative media; you only have to scroll through your social media feeds to get a sense of this, so do protect yourself and limit your time online. We know it has its place, but you need to be in charge of managing your exposure to it.

Putting this into practice

This goes back to planning your day and making the most of every minute. I find it useful to plan my day in advance and use a timer when going online, which helps me to keep focused and not to get drawn into unnecessary negative content online. Use your time wisely, do your research and keep focused, and this will really help you keep positive.

Ignore whiners and complainers

I'm getting better at managing my contact with whiners and complainers! I have a fairly positive and upbeat personality, so I really struggle with spending too much time with people who inherently see the negative in every situation. Be mindful of people's attitudes, and protect yourself. This will really help preserve and cultivate your own positive attitude.

Putting this into practice

As a business owner, your working week is precious, and you don't want to spoil it spending time with negative people. I would suggest arranging 1-2-1s with people before or at the end of a networking meeting, and always give the meetings a start and end time. This will help protect your time and make the meetings more focused and positive. If you get the feeling that someone is quite negative, try to take control of the meeting's agenda and steer it to a close as quickly as you can. Having online meetings via Zoom or Skype is a good way to keep positive, and you can always find a way to bring a meeting to a close rapidly. Remember, motivational speaker Jim Rohn said that, "you are the average of the five people you hang around with," so if you interact with negative people consistently, you're more likely to pick up this way of thinking, which reinforces the need to avoid spending time with whingers!

Use a more positive vocabulary

This is a useful technique. It's worthwhile listening to your own use of words and language. If you notice you don't use a 'glass is half full' vocabulary, now is the time to address it and purposely try to use more upbeat language. This will have a big impact on your attitude, and not just at work.

Putting this into practice

Try to be aware of your language when you're motivating your team. Pick your words carefully, as they will quickly pick up your energy. When speaking to prospective clients, be aware of the words you use. Really try to relate to their issues, and explain in a positive way how you and your team can make a difference.

So, with all these tips in mind, you can undoubtedly see the importance of having a positive mindset when you're running your own business and when you're the boss. I'm sure you can recognise people you know, some of whom display a negative mindset and others of whom display a positive mindset, and I bet I know who you would rather spend more time with! It's easier than you think to adopt a more positive mindset, and the benefits of this attitude will be far-reaching. Here are some easy to implement examples: get up immediately and avoid the snooze button; drink more water to keep hydrated; enjoy daily exercise; eat a good breakfast; and maybe even meditate. Making simple changes to your daily routine will really help you feel in control and provide you with a more positive outlook; give it a try.

When things do go wrong in your life, having a positive mindset can really help with how you deal with these situations.

Here are some tips on how to deal with tricky times, all of which benefit from your positive attitude:

» Think of similar difficulties that resulted in a positive outcome in the end.

» Brainstorm ideas to help you get out of a difficult scenario.

» Choose the solution that sounds the most effective, and remind yourself of the baby steps needed to reach the end result.

» Take action and do something about your problem rather than wallowing in a negative state.

» Focus on the solution rather than the problem; don't lose hope!

» Avoid negative self-talk; maintaining a positive attitude all the time can be tricky, but if you believe in yourself, you can do it. This is where being part of a franchise, for example, really helps; you can share how you're feeling and get the support that you need.

» And, finally, believe in yourself; this is easier said than done sometimes, but with practice and with a positive mindset, this becomes the norm, and you'll naturally find an opportunity in every difficulty.

The need for discipline

A common fear when starting to work for yourself is the worry that you won't be disciplined enough or that you may well start off OK, but the novelty might wear off after a few months, and you could find yourself more interested in stacking the dishwasher than writing a business pitch.

As we already discussed, having a positive mindset and a winning attitude will both help with keeping you on track in your business. We provide our new franchisees with a bespoke induction that covers everything from setting up a business bank account through to effectively marketing their franchise, networking and signing up clients. As part of the induction, the new franchisees get to meet existing franchisees, who share best practice, and members of the team who are delivering the client work. A common thread that runs through the induction is the need to have discipline. Most of the team have never worked from home before, so we provide good training on the best ways to set up and run their business effectively. We look at everyone's personality type and help them develop a good plan, so they get the most out of their working week.

Our support and training doesn't stop after the induction; we're a constant support to our team, and we have regular monthly calls too. We recognise that the summer holidays, for example, can be quite disruptive for the team, with children off school and clients going on holiday, so we look to the wider team to offer holiday cover and we help the franchisees come up with a realistic plan to support them through this busy time. Flexibility lies at the root of our business, so we understand that being disciplined is a key driver in our franchise's success.

 Now, fear not, these tips should reassure you that there are a number of ways to keep on track with both your work and time keeping, which you will really benefit from when running your own business, even from the kitchen table.

Let's look at how we can put these tips into practice when running your franchise:

✓ Establish a designated working space

This doesn't mean that you have to dedicate a whole room to your office, but it's a good idea to have a specific area where you work from that sets the tone. It would be great to have a sunny area with as few distractions as possible. Remember, you can vary where you work – you could pop to a coffee shop or hot desk somewhere too – but it's good to have a regular space that you associate with work at home. My home office has an orange wall to highlight our branding, our logo on the wall (which works really well when I have online calls), and I also have a standing desk, but this is all after having run the business for nine years! I've always used a separate space from the rest of the house, though, as I really value the boundary between home and work. Our local hotel has always been a useful place for me to meet business connections, as it hasn't always been appropriate to meet them in my own home.

✓ Dress appropriately

It's known fact that there is a psychological benefit to being dressed for purpose, so it's advisable not to sit at your home desk in your PJs every day, however tempting it is! Of course, there will be times when you're in the flow and still in your PJs, but getting dressed for work helps with your work mindset and is useful for your Skype calls too, although I've been known to do a Zoom call online wearing a business shirt and my joggers! Work wear has changed over the last few years too, and as long as you look smart and appropriate for your audience that is fine; sometimes, I'll wear smart trainers for a client meeting or networking, and I always wear slippers at home as it helps me feel relaxed, which is important.

✓ Have a timetable

Setting yourself a timetable for the day is a great way to educate friends and family that you're still working a professional day. If you get to work on time – even if the commute is a 10-second walk – this will really help you start your day in the right way. It will help to set the boundary between work and leisure time, and it will help you avoid getting distracted and putting the washing on. You can happily timetable washing, etc. into your daily calendar, but this needs to be done with purpose rather than in an idle way because the washing machine caught your eye suddenly. I use a focus timer app that follows the Pomodoro technique, which breaks working activities down into 25-minute slots separated by short breaks; it works a treat.

✓ Write and action a to-do list

A to-do list plays an important part in your daily timetable. It's useful to prioritise tasks and review your list at the end of each day. It's good to assess your productivity and set a new list at the end of the day for the following one. A to-do list will help focus your mind too, which is very important. As well as the good old-fashioned pen-and-paper to-do list, which I favour, there are a number of online options that are worth considering; e.g. Wunderlist, Todoist, Trello and Evernote.

✓ Have daily rituals

As well as having a focused to-do list, it's a good idea to build in some daily rituals and routines. For example, at the start of every day, I'll look at LinkedIn for 15 minutes, and make comments on posts, engage with others and connect with new people. This has now become a habit as I do it every morning.

✓ Set the tone and boundaries for communication

There are so many methods that we can use for communicating remotely: phone calls, texts, emails, Skype/Zoom, etc. It's inevitable that you'll have a favourite method, but it's useful to vary your communication and work out if, for example, a phone call is more efficient than numerous emails pinging back and forth. It's great to have a choice, and they each have their pros and cons. Remember that you can put your phone on silent or pause email notifications too, which all helps with concentration and time management. We have a monthly franchise call using Zoom, and the franchisees love it as they can all see each other, and it's a great way to chat and learn in an open environment.

✓ Take breaks

It's useful to factor in breaks during the day and to purposefully have time out, as you would if you were working in a corporate office. Don't have lunch at your desk. You must have time to switch off, so popping out for a walk, going into the kitchen and making lunch are all activities that will allow you to refocus.

✓ Get out from behind your desk

It's worth factoring in some face-to-face meetings during the week, as this will naturally break up your week and also enable you to have some live human interaction! Examples of this could be having a client meeting, going networking, visiting an exhibition or even working in a coffee shop.

In this section, we've covered a lot of points around the importance of being disciplined in your work, from setting a timetable to being clear about your vision for the business. As part of the Get Ahead franchise, we give excellent training on how to achieve this balance and to get the flexibility you deserve alongside running a successful and professional business.

Case study – A day in the life of regional director Geri

From doing to running your business

It's now a good time to really look into the role of a regional director in more detail. A great way to do this is to understand what a typical day is like for a franchisee, so here goes:

7am   I wake up and sort out the kids (remembering my mindset here, saying a *positive affirmation*, reviewing my timetable for the day and following my daily routine, including having 10 minutes to focus on the day ahead before kick-starting my day – all avoiding any technology!). I display a winning focus and winning attitude.

8.30am   I review my to-do list (remembering that if I'm putting something off I'll do it first, so I'll feel so much better when it's done).

I check social media, and I respond to any messages and mentions.

I get my networking pitch ready.

9.30am	I drive to the networking meeting, listening to a podcast on the way. Audible is a great way to listen to podcasts and audio books. This is really good use of dead time, and it's useful to reflect on what I've learnt at the end of the journey and try to take one nugget of learning away with me.
10am	I arrive at networking and make the most of the free networking at the start of the meeting. I have some positive conversations with people I haven't met before, showcasing a winning mindset. I ask questions and show a genuine interest in others. At the end of the meeting, I collate all the business cards and I'm clear who I need to connect with on LinkedIn.
12pm	I have my 1-2-1 meeting with a prospective client.
1.00pm	I take an al fresco lunch break in the garden.
1.30pm	I'm back at my desk for the team Zoom call, to check in on progress with my team and review our latest project. Communicating and being clear on next steps is vital, and this displays a winning attitude to the team.
2pm	I post photos from the networking meeting on LinkedIn, with a thank you to the host and tagging relevant people.
	I finish off my new client proposal and email it over. I respond to other emails from the day.
3.15pm	I walk to school to collect the kids.
4pm	Once back home, I write a to-do list for tomorrow with key actions, and I confirm meetings.
4.30pm	I take time off with the family.

7pm   I drive to a networking meeting, remembering my badge and business cards.

10pm   I'm back home and ready for bed!

This typical day showcases how Geri the franchisee had a good balance between working from home, dealing with her team and getting face-to-face contact. This was all helped by her discipline and her ability to stick to her timetable and make the most of every minute. You can easily see how – with a positive mindset and an organised attitude – a franchisee can achieve such a lot and still get time with their family too.

KEY TAKEAWAYS

Mindset

It's important to develop and maintain a positive mindset when running your own business. To succeed at running your own business, it's crucial that you apply this mindset to all aspects of your business. Remember Jeff Keller's (2012) tips on how to cultivate a positive attitude:

- ✓ Remember that *you* control your attitude
- ✓ Adopt beliefs that frame events in a positive way
- ✓ Create a library of positive thoughts
- ✓ Avoid angry or negative media
- ✓ Ignore whiners and complainers
- ✓ Use a more positive vocabulary

Self-esteem, drive and discipline

Remember the role of healthy self-esteem and how you can put this into practice when running your own business, by being capable of making your own decisions, regardless of what everyone else is doing. Formulating a winning mindset keeps you focused and acknowledges that, whatever obstacles get in your way, you'll succeed in the end. Drive, determination and passion are a winning combination too in helping you make changes for the better, and concentrating on these key areas will really benefit you and your business. Being authentic is critical, and this will shine through in all that you do. A common fear when starting to work for yourself is the worry that you won't be disciplined enough. Remember our tips for helping you keep on track: having a designated working space, dressing appropriately and working to a bespoke timetable every day. Writing and actioning a to-do list really helps you focus, and having daily rituals keeps you on track. Communicating effectively can work wonders, as does taking breaks and getting out from behind your desk.

Hopefully, the case study of Geri has helped you see how all of this information is put into practice.

CHAPTER 6

How to Make It Successful

By now, you'll have established that working for yourself is a really attractive option. You want to run your own business, be in charge of your work-life balance and have a business you can be proud of. A business that can grow with you and scale over time. Hopefully, you can see that our franchise opportunity could be the perfect solution for you.

In this chapter, we're going to look at the following:

✓ Getting in the right mindset – a reminder

✓ Choosing the right franchise option for you

✓ Making it successful

✓ Scaling up – how big do you want to get?

Getting the right mindset – a reminder

Once again, you need to remember that mindset plays a huge part in how you feel about running your own business and being a business owner. It's essential to develop and maintain a positive mindset, and cultivate a positive attitude, which we looked at closely in the previous chapter.

A positive attitude is important for ensuring that you have a fulfilling and enjoyable life, both personally and professionally. Building a positive attitude will make it easier for you to recognise and reflect on positive emotions as you experience them. You'll also start reframing negative emotions in the moment that they begin to occur.

To be a competent boss and to run your own business successfully, you need to demonstrate a positive outlook that shines consistently through everything you do, even when things don't quite go to plan.

Some examples of this could be the following:

Handling a tricky client who is complaining that a VA hasn't done a good enough job

Your approach

Accept that the client is always right! Thank them for letting you know they have an issue and explain what you'll do to put this right (e.g. you'll speak to the VA); you might suggest providing the client with an alternative VA, etc. This will all be carried out with a smile on your face and in a relaxed and calm manner (even if you aren't feeling quite this way at the time!).

Your internet goes down unexpectedly and you're on a tight deadline

Your approach

Rather than instinctively seeing this as a major issue, try to work offline as much as you can, and then finish this work off at a friend's house or local café where the Wi-Fi is strong as well as the coffee!

Your children are home from school suddenly and you have a lot of follow up calls to make

Your approach

Go through your list, prioritise the calls, and then communicate with your children to explain what you need them to do in order for you to get through your calls without interruption. Everyone benefits from clear communication.

Also, if you have systems in place that can help when things go wrong – and remembering that plan B is just as effective as plan A – then when you need to use an alternative route, you're not completely thrown off track and you're ready to handle a difficult situation. As with many things, the more times you practise solving tricky situations with a positive mindset, the easier they become.

So, now we've quickly recapped this most useful trait, let's look in more detail about how working with us and our franchise could be your future.

Who's who – a reminder

» Regional director / franchisee – *you*

» Client – busy business owner

» Team member – VA (sourced from within the Get Ahead agency or one you've sourced yourself locally)

You might find the picture on page 73 a useful visual.

Choosing the right franchise option for you

There are two ways to run your Get Ahead franchise:

1. Solo

2. In a partnership

Going solo (as a franchisee/you)

Going solo as a franchisee simply means buying the franchise yourself and being solely in charge. We've discussed different ways to set up your own franchise in Chapter 4: either as a sole trader, where you're in business on your own, are self-employed, and you and the business are one and the same; or as a limited company, where the business is separate and you're the director.

Main benefits:

✓ Sole decision-maker

When making a decision about your business, you don't have to consult anyone else, but you have the freedom to decide what you want to do and how you do it (as long as this is within franchise guidelines!), so you have autonomy, which is power.

✓ Freedom

You have the opportunity to work with whomever you want; you don't need to consult anyone, and this freedom is really motivating.

✓ Ability to grow your business

Running your own franchise gives you the ability to grow the business and focus on it without any interruptions. You can give the business its own personality that is unique to you. For example, Jo – who runs our South Yorkshire franchise – has a background in HR, so she's able to talk comfortably about this service to her clients, and we've benefited as a business from now being able to offer HR as a support service across the business as a whole.

Drawbacks:

✕ Isolating

Some people say they wouldn't have the confidence to run their own business, as they find it isolating and lonely because they're the sole decision-maker. (Actually, as part of a franchise, you have the opportunity to share ideas and get advice from the other franchisees and from me too, so you're actually never alone!)

✕ Challenging

When you come up against challenges in the business (e.g. a tricky client or team member) not having a partner to discuss this with could be hard work (this is when you would fall back on your fellow franchisees or me).

✕ Large territory

Your territory within your network is pretty large, so you could feel that you have a lot of untapped region to still network and market to, which could be quite daunting.

✕ Risk

Running the business on your own could put you at risk if you become ill or need to take time off, as you don't have a business partner to support you (this is when you could tap into the franchise support and get back up from nearby franchisees).

Solo-franchisee success toolkit

At Get Ahead, we understand and know about these issues, so we've worked hard to make sure that franchisees aren't overwhelmed or daunted at the start of their Get Ahead journey. Here are some of the keys to success:

Clear objectives

We work closely with you to set realistic monthly KPIs, so you're clear on what to measure in your business (e.g. number of networking meetings attended, number of prospective clients, number of proposals sent out, where your prospects are coming from and your LinkedIn activity).

Planning your marketing

As a franchisee, you're automatically given access to fresh marketing content, which is updated weekly. This is a huge asset and can be used to boost your own regional marketing. Connecting with your potential clients (busy business owners) online is critical, as is consistent communication, so you'll need to factor time into your week to promote your franchise online and offline.

Networking

Networking is a key activity that you'll need to embrace to promote your franchise in your territory. When you launch your business, you'll be encouraged to visit a wide range of different networking meetings, online and offline, and your aim is to find a couple that you'll want to join and commit to attending on a regular basis. Networking is a sure way to meet like-minded business owners and to start developing key relationships within your business community, which both help to promote your business and to start reaching out to prospective clients.

Client management

Once you've started signing up clients and matching them with the appropriate team members (VAs), you'll need to manage this process and make sure that your clients are happy with the support they're receiving. It's essential that you keep connected with them and provide a consistent level of service.

Team

As we've already mentioned, a huge positive of being part of our franchise is that you can get up and running from day one, as you have access to our large central pool of VAs, who are available to support your clients. This is an amazing benefit, as it means you can always find the right VA for the job!

As a new franchisee launching with us, you'll have a bespoke induction spread over a few days. This includes running through our franchise manual, meeting the core members of the team (a VA who will explain examples of the work they do and your fellow franchisees), having photographs taken that will be used for your press release and in our marketing, and having a video made that will go on to your individual page on our website. Our franchisees always welcome this induction, and it marks the start of your journey with us.

We're hugely interactive, and regular communication and mentoring is at the heart of all that we do, from 1-2-1s to our monthly franchise calls. We're incredibly aware that our franchisees need our support from day one, but this doesn't end after your induction; far from it! You're business owners in your own right, but with the added support and security of a trusted network around you whenever you need it; this is a win-win for sure.

Remind yourself of the case study I shared in Chapter 4.

Working in a partnership

Another option for running our franchise is to run it as a partnership with a friend. Our teams in Newcastle and Berkshire are both run as partnerships. Buying the franchise with a friend can be a fantastic experience that strengthens your friendship, as well as enabling you to realise your dream of running your own business. But, as with any business venture, it isn't without risks. Buying this franchise with a friend means that you have someone to share the upfront financial investment and the ongoing business responsibilities with, and to celebrate success with. But things can go wrong if one partner isn't contributing as much as the other or expects different things from the business.

Main benefits:

✓ Spreading the risk

You don't have to fund the initial franchise investment or ongoing business costs by yourself. Costs are shared between you, reducing your personal financial commitment.

✓ Having back up

By sharing a franchise with a friend, you can cover for each other when you need back up. Especially, as a working parent, if your kids are ill or you're on holiday, work can still go ahead without you.

✓ Increasing your impact

With two franchisees, you can have twice the impact at events. Your stronger presence can make you more memorable and allow you to make more quality connections in a shorter period of time.

✓ Supporting each other

Running the franchise can be lonely, particularly when not running your business from home or not employing your own staff. Buying the franchise with a friend means that you're not alone, but you're part of your own unique team.

Drawbacks:

✗ Confusion and duplication

Do you both have exactly the same approach to pricing, communication and deadlines? Do you both know exactly what you do? You may end up confusing clients if they don't have one clear point of contact who is giving them consistent information.

✕ You're not completely in charge

You have to consider someone else's point of view and can't take important decisions without consulting your franchise partner. You may have to compromise, especially on big decisions.

✕ Differences of opinion, objectives, ambitions, etc.

You might not always have the same time to devote to the business or the same objectives for it. You might not agree on your approach to new business development or marketing costs. You'll need to find a way to resolve these differences to make the partnership work.

Joint-franchisee success toolkit

At Get Ahead, we've worked hard to make sure that our franchisees who are operating as a partnership are fully prepared for how it will be when running their business together. Here are some of the keys to success:

Choose your friend wisely

You may have lots of great friends, but not many whom you could comfortably share your business with. Consider whether it's the franchise business that feels right for you or working with a friend that is drawing you towards an opportunity. When buying a franchise with a friend, both the friend and the franchise opportunity need to be right.

Enjoy working together

For some people, running their own franchise can be lonely, but with a co-franchisee, you immediately have someone who is in the same boat as you, who understands your challenges and successes, and who can support you all the way. If you choose to share the franchise with someone with similar values, you're likely to have the same ambitions, aspirations and approach to success, and can enjoy starting and growing your business together.

Share the workload, the skills, the responsibilities, etc.

Defining distinct roles for each of you means that, unlike many franchisees, you don't have to be the chief executive officer (CEO), sales director, finance manager and HR all rolled into one. Each of you can assume the responsibilities most suited to your background or interests. If you and your friend have complementary skills, you have a solid foundation for running a business that is over and above having a gap if you don't possess all the skills yourself.

Be accountable to someone else

The fantastic thing about a franchise partnership is that there is always someone there to keep you focused and motivated. Consider blocking time for tasks that you need to work on together, as well as for business strategy meetings. Set clear objectives for each day/week/month/year, to ensure you know what each other is working on and therefore support each other.

Maintain your independence

Buying this franchise with a friend doesn't mean that it's all you ever talk about 24/7. To make your partnership a success, you need to enjoy working together as well as working apart. This helps maintain the friendship as well as the business partnership. It also allows you to embrace your own personal style of working and your personal strengths.

Set boundaries

Do your business in work time and your social connection in personal time. Find ways to accommodate both parts of your lives effectively. For example, a walk first thing on the days when you work together allows the social bit to be done, as well as focusing on a task list for the day. Keep work out of social get-togethers, so that you can still be 'just friends' and switch off from work.

Give feedback

It's so important to give your fellow franchisee feedback. Say thank you when your partner has helped you out or made a difference. Don't just assume that, just because they share your franchise, they share your thought processes. It's vital to vocalise your appreciation for what they do, as well as ways in which you think you could work better together.

Be open and honest

Before you buy the franchise with a friend, talk about the risks and the consequences. What happens if it takes off? What happens if it goes wrong? What if one of you wants out? If you can't be open and honest with each other from the start, then you might need to reconsider your business partnership.

Respect each other

To work together effectively, you have to be aligned in your thinking, your processes and your efforts. You need to be 50/50 all the way, and you must understand that there is always give and take, which you should accept without judging. Believe in yourselves and the fact that you can achieve more together than you could alone.

Case study – Clare & Alison

Here's a case study of our franchisees who run our franchise as a partnership

Clare and Alison are the joint regional directors of our Bristol office, and they know just what it's like to set up a new business as a partnership. They've been friends for over 14 years and have worked together previously. They've always wanted to work for themselves and, after researching their franchise option, they felt that running a Get Ahead regional office was the perfect platform.

There are so many reasons to go into business as a partnership – it can bring all sorts of benefits and a few extra challenges – so they're here to tell you what to expect, from their experience.

> Clare stated, *"One of the biggest upsides to starting a business as a pair is that you always have someone there who's going through the same thing as you, and who can offer support and motivation along the way. You can also play to each other's strengths – our working styles really complement each other, and that's been a huge part of making our business a success."*

Another advantage is that you can scale the business more quickly due to the simple fact that there are two of you! That means twice as much networking, twice as many phone calls and twice as many ideas to help the business grow.

Of course, for all this to work, it's crucial to find the right person to go into business with. For Alison and Clare, going into business together made a lot of sense. They'd met at their previous workplace, so they were colleagues first and then became friends. Whoever you're thinking about starting a business with, it's really important that you give your relationship that professional grounding first. If you haven't worked together before, try to collaborate on some smaller projects to find out if your working styles are going to gel.

You should also remember that working together means *working together*, so if you're likely to distract each other all day, then you might not make the best business partners! A business partner is someone who you can work next to quietly, and who can wait to chat until break times or after work.

Alison confirmed, *"Get Ahead has enabled me to fulfil my dream of running my own business, but I have the added support of working closely with Clare and the wider support of the Get Ahead team – it's the best of both worlds, really."*

As you already know, a Get Ahead franchise gets plenty of support (including training and mentorship) and comes with the knowledge that you're part of a bigger, national team. But having another person working with you every day provides an extra level of confidence that is just invaluable. For Clare and Alison, this has been the perfect solution, so if you're thinking of opening a Get Ahead regional office as a pair, Clare and Alison say, "Go for it!"

"Being a regional director for Get Ahead is a hugely rewarding job, and I love the flexibility of the working hours and the variety of every day. I also love the ability to really scale the business by adding new regional team members as I need them. I would recommend it to anyone who's thinking of taking the plunge," Alison added.

> Hence, those are the two ways you can become a franchisee with Get Ahead. Depending on your situation and level of commitment, going solo or with a partnership offers flexible solutions for any person wanting to run their own business, without being completely on their own (even if it's a solo franchise, there is support!).

 Let's now take a quick look at how you can make your franchise successful. Without this next step, you don't have a business, and although this book isn't a guide on how to run your franchise, this is a good taster of what you'll need to do to get the business running profitably.

Making it successful

Obviously, we give full training to our franchisees on how to set up your franchise, but clients are clearly the biggest factor in making your franchise succeed, so let's now take a look at your ideal client base and how you can find them.

But before we get into the fine detail, let's first look at why a client may need your services as opposed to going to work with a VA directly. (This is probably going to be the biggest barrier between using you and your clients finding their own VA, so it's good to know the key reasons why using Get Ahead could be an advantage to your client.)

You're running a virtual outsourcing agency, so your clients (busy business owners) will immediately be attracted to the breadth of services that you can provide them. They will be aware that you have a number of different experts (VAs) offering a variety of support services, rather than one person with limited hours available. Your clients will understand that you're the connector between identifying what support *they* need and finding the best person or people for the job.

Another benefit of working with an agency is that, even if the VA is on holiday or off sick, your client will have seamless support, as another VA from the team can cover the work and provide the continuous support needed.

Being able to explain the differences between your services and the client going and hiring someone directly will help you secure more business. It's important to get this aspect clear before you start talking to potential clients.

What type of clients are best?

Working with the right clients is crucial to any business. You want to be able to market your services to the right audience, so that the sale is easy and appropriate. The last thing you want is to have to do a hard sell or start discounting your services just to get a sale.

Attributes of your perfect client

The perfect clients for your Get Ahead franchise are people who have set up their own business and have realised that, in order to scale it effectively, they need to start to let go of some of the tasks that are holding them back, or are start-ups who understand from the word go that they can't do it all themselves. Initially, when someone sets up a business, they're involved in absolutely everything from admin and accounts through to marketing and PR. However, this level of involvement isn't sustainable for growing the business effectively. This is where you come in! You can work with the business owner and help them identify a number of tasks that they either aren't good at or that are holding them back. These tasks are then handed over to a member of your team, who will carry out the work for your client.

Here are a few attributes of your perfect clients:

- ✓ Have a primary focus on growth (for start-ups)
- ✓ Recognise that outsourcing is better than employing someone
- ✓ Have the budget to use us
- ✓ Are open-minded enough to recognise that outside help is needed

Before we look at where to find your ideal clients, let's have a fast recap of who's who, and what we mean by territories or regions:

- » Client – the busy business owner
- » Regional director – you, the franchisee
- » VA – one of your team, who will carry out the work for your client
- » Territory/region – the defined area in which you operate your franchise; we use sophisticated mapping software that produces a clear territory with specific postcodes

Finding your perfect clients

There are a number of different ways for you to source your perfect clients, and we're going to look at few in more detail now:

- » **Referrals or introductions**

We've been in business since 2010, so we're well established, and people recognise our brand. Naturally, we get introduced to potential clients by existing clients who love what we do, by people we know and even by ex-clients who no longer need our support. Referrals are very precious, and we really value these, as the prospect already knows a little about what we do and the sales process is already simple. Referrals and introductions need to be treated as gold from the very beginning, and it's essential that you thank the person who has introduced us too. It's also worth looking at who you can team up with locally who would possibly also work with your ideal clients (the busy business owners) (e.g. accountants, bookkeepers or business coaches) and you could refer clients to each other.

» Direct enquiries

Every franchisee (regional director / *you*) has a dedicated page on our website, which showcases your details. This is your webpage, and you can direct people to this page in your marketing. There is also an enquiry form on the website, which prospective clients (busy business owners) can complete if they're interested in your services, and this information is then passed on to you.

» Networking meetings

It's essential for a franchisee to feel comfortable and confident enough to attend a networking meeting, and to be able to talk about their business to other people. (We looked at this earlier in the chapter, but it's such an important way of getting clients, it's worth repeating, as it'll be a big part of your marketing.) I'm not expecting a top-class acting job here! I just need you to be professional and keen to meet new people. I see these networking meetings as an essential part of your week, in which you'll meet like-minded business owners, learn new things and, hopefully, meet some potential clients too. At your induction, we provide you with full training on how to get the most out of networking, including what to say and how to say it! It's crucial that you're networking with your ideal clients, so understanding where they hang out is really important. It's also worth considering trade shows, exhibitions and online meet-ups too.

» Social media

As a business, we have over 17,000 followers across our social media platforms at time of writing, and you'll benefit from this activity as soon as you launch. We're constantly sharing relevant articles and showcasing case studies that demonstrate our expertise in flexible working. LinkedIn is a personal favourite of mine, and I love engaging daily with a wide variety of people on there. We find that a number of our clients are also active on social media, so it's vital for us as a business to have a strong and engaging profile, meaning prospective clients will notice us and will be encouraged to get in touch with us via social media too.

» **Email marketing**

We provide you (our franchisee) with a monthly newsletter that is sent out to your own regional email list. Once you launch your business, you're encouraged to start building an email list of prospective clients and people you meet networking. It's amazing how effective these emails are at reminding people about your wide range of services. Our franchisees (regional directors) love these emails too, as we send them out on their behalf; they just give us their contact list, and the job is done for them! This is another huge benefit of being part of our franchise, as opposed to doing everything yourself.

» **Exhibitions or trade shows**

Exhibitions are an effective way to promote your services and help find new clients too. Normally, there are annual business exhibitions in every city, and these innately attract busy business owners needing help. We encourage every franchisee to exhibit once a year, and we'll help by giving you some money towards the exhibition cost. Exhibitions are also great places to meet new people and to expand your local networking connections.

» **PR support**

When a new franchisee launches with us, we produce a bespoke PR launch package for them. This includes a press release that our PR manager sends out to the local press to tell them about you and your new franchise. As a business, we also respond regularly to requests from journalists for examples and case studies, which is an effective way to educate more people about our flexible support, and it helps us reach new clients in turn.

I hope you're now clearer about our exciting franchise opportunity to be a regional director? That is, the opportunity to manage a virtual team and support busy business owners who need specific help to grow *their* businesses. The ability to scale your own business is huge, as there are so many busy business owners in desperate need of skilled support, and we'll help you build a flexible business to provide this support.

Scaling up – how big do you want it to get?

The beauty of running a Get Ahead franchise is that your business is totally scalable. As a regional director, you're running a defined geographical territory, and the number of clients you can support is unlimited because you use VAs from our core team to carry out the client work. This is our strong point of difference, because from day one you have access to a large pool of VAs who are ready to support your clients. The core team is extremely broad, from people to answer phones through to social media managers and marketing experts. Over time, it makes sense for you to start to build a team of local VAs who can meet you and your clients face to face when needed. Although the support you provide is remote, your clients will like to meet up face to face from time to time – there's nothing better than this for cementing working relationships – so you're encouraged to look for local VAs to join your own regional team. You may well meet potential team members at networking meetings and through recommendations. Your new team members will also speak to me at the start, so I can bring them up to speed on the business, our core values and future plans. Exciting!

A brief overview of how regions work.

As we've already mentioned, you get a defined geographical territory (also known as a region) when you launch your franchise. This territory is bespoke to you, and only you can operate a Get Ahead franchise in that area. We use advanced territory-mapping software to define your ideal region. The software overlays postcodes on to a map, and we then look at the number of businesses that are active in these different postcodes, so we're all happy that you have a sufficient number of businesses to market to in your territory. When a potential client makes an enquiry to us, we always ask where they're based, and we can then allocate them to the relevant franchisee based on their postcode.

I love that our growing franchise family members are non-competitive and super supportive of each other. We've built a community that supports flexible working for the team, our clients and for the business as a whole; this is a common thread that binds us all together. We're in this together.

Owning a Get Ahead franchise provides you with the support that you need, and I'm sure that, by now, you're seeing the opportunity it offers in terms of flexibility and scalability.
Get in touch if you want to learn more about how you can do this (email office@getaheadva.com or call 01483 332220).

KEY TAKEAWAYS

- **Choosing the right franchise model**
  In this chapter, we've reviewed the different ways to set up your Get Ahead business: solo or as a partnership. The most popular option is to run the franchise on your own, but it's useful to know that it can be operated successfully in a partnership. You need to choose the best option for you, to play to your strengths.

- **Understanding that clients are the soul of your business and how to find them**
  We've looked at your ideal client (the busy business owner) and how you can market to them. It's all about getting the right mix of marketing activity and making sure that you're consistent and saying the same thing, wherever and whenever you show up. There are many ways to meet and establish connections with busy business owners, and we've covered all of these:

  » Referrals or introductions

  » Direct enquiries

» Networking meetings

» Social media

» Email marketing

» Exhibitions or trade shows

» PR support

- **Scaling up is an opportunity for growth**
  Our franchise model is based on the opportunity for you to scale and grow by outsourcing the client work to our growing team of VAs from day one. This means that you don't have to turn clients away, and you can utilise our core team of VAs when you first start with us and grow your own regional support team over time too. This is really exciting and a huge bonus of being part of our Get Ahead family.

CHAPTER 7

𝓕𝓐𝓠𝓼

I thought this chapter would be helpful as it captures the questions we often get asked by potential franchisees, and I imagine that you may well be thinking of some of these too!

Of course, you can get in touch with me for more information by calling 01483 332220 or emailing office@getaheadva.com.

» **What is the cost to set up the business after I've paid the franchise fee?**

There is minimal cost to start running your business, other than needing access to a laptop/PC, a mobile phone and a car to travel to events. You'll need a cash buffer of around £1,000 to cover networking fees and to be able to pay your team whilst waiting for payment from clients in the early days. Our clients pay us within seven days, and we pay our team within three working days, which is a huge benefit to our team as they don't have to worry about invoicing clients, etc.

» **Are there options to spread out the payment of the franchise fee?**

There are some great finance options for spreading out the franchise fee payment, and I will happily give you more information on these.

» **How do I get my clients?**

In your induction, we will share our best practices for promoting your business and finding your ideal clients. Networking is a proven way to connect with people who will need your support. Our website and social media platforms also drive enquiries too.

» **Do I get my own website?**

Every franchisee has their own dedicated page on our website, which shows your photos, a video of you, and information about your business and where you're based.

» **Do I get my own landline number?**

Every franchisee is given a local telephone number that appears on the website and on your business cards, and it is answered by our team, so you don't have to worry about missing a call!

» **Do I print my own business cards and marketing materials?**

At launch, you're given an allocation of business cards and rate cards. When these have run out, you can get them reprinted by a supplier of your choice, and the cost of this is covered by you.

» **Do I need my own office to run the franchise?**

It's advisable for you to have a dedicated workspace, but this can easily be within your own home. In our experience, there is no need to rent an office. We've looked at how to get the most out of working from home in Chapter 5. There are also co-working spaces in many towns, which give a good balance between being on your own and being in an office environment. You would need to pay for the cost of this, so bear that in mind.

» How do I find VAs to support my clients?

From day one, you'll have access to our core group of VAs. I can help you match the best VA with the job, and we're constantly adding new team members. Over time, you'll want to build a small team who are local to you, so you can meet them face to face too, but there is no rush for this to happen.

» Do I get a specific territory within which to work?

We use sophisticated territory-mapping software to plan a bespoke territory for each franchisee. We take into account where you live, and your nearest towns, and overlay data that shows us how many businesses with one to four employees are active in these places, so you'll have a great idea of where to network and market your services. Our territories are all of a similar size and offer great opportunities to reach your ideal clients.

» What happens if there is already a franchise running where I live?

In this instance, we would look at where else you could set up, within reasonable distance of your home. You would work from home anyway, so that wouldn't be an issue; you would just need to be able to travel to relevant events in your territory.

» I have a lot of contacts around the UK, can I tell them about my new business?

We encourage you to tell everyone you know about your new business! When I launched in 2010, my first two clients came via a friend, so this a great way to market your new venture. If you're already connected to someone who wants you to support them, but they're based in an area where we already have a franchisee, then it's common courtesy to tell our other franchisee and ask for their approval. However, if you go networking and meet someone who is based in another territory, then you're obliged to introduce them to the relevant franchisee. Our franchisees are extremely supportive and non-competitive, and good, clear communication supports this ethos.

» **When can I expect to make money?**

We have a forecasting model that we share with all prospective franchisees that plainly shows the earning potential of your franchise, based on an average number of clients and hours worked. There is a huge opportunity to make money within six months of starting your business, as long as you're getting a good pipeline of clients and are networking consistently. We predict that, with a team of four VAs supporting your clients with an average of 100 billed hours per month, by the end of your year one you can make a £10,000 margin in that year, rising to £50,000 by year five with a team of 12. These figures are based on you working part-time school hours.

» **Do I need to be VAT registered?**

All our franchisees are VAT registered, as this provides consistency across our company. Your accountant can advise you on the best VAT options for you.

» **Can I run the franchise with a friend?**

There is an option to run the franchise as a partnership with someone else, and this is covered in more detail in Chapter 6. You need to think carefully about who to choose when selecting someone to be your partner, but there are many benefits too!

» **Can I do some of the client work myself?**

As a franchisee, you're encouraged to outsource the work that your clients need help with to your team of VAs to free you up to spend your time networking and growing your connections. However, if you have a specialist skill (e.g. marketing strategy or HR) then you can happily provide this support to your clients.

» **What career background makes for the best franchisee?**

Our franchisees come from a variety of backgrounds, but what they all have in common is the ability to listen, ask questions, be interested in others, and have the skills needed to lead and manage a team. Ideal backgrounds are sales, marketing, HR or operations, but these aren't exclusive. Your induction with us is bespoke, so if there is a specific area that you feel you need support with (e.g. public-speaking training), then we'll give you the necessary training and guidance.

> » **What happens if I need to sell my franchise within the five years?**

You can sell your franchise before the end of the five years. We would need to work together to market the opportunity, and I would be heavily involved in the recruitment process. If we managed to find the perfect replacement franchisee, then you would receive payment minus the time it takes to train them.

> » **What happens at the end of the five-year franchise agreement?**

At the end of five years of trading, we can simply reissue the agreement, though we'll need to cover the legal costs to enter into a new agreement. There is no additional franchise fee.

> » **What happens if I decide to leave, and I've brought in one or more new VAs? Do they come with me?**

Your team of VAs are freelancers, so it's totally up to them if they choose to still work with Get Ahead once you've left.

Conclusion

Well done! You've made it through to the end of my book!

There is a lot to take in throughout this book, but I hope that the content has been written in a logical sequence. As I mentioned in the introduction to this book, I'm passionate about providing flexible working, having experienced a lack of similar opportunities when I was needing them most.

Our franchisees love the work that they do: "I love being a Get Ahead franchisee, as I can run my own business as part of a supportive and collaborative team, flexibly around my family," says Fiona Ibbetson, regional director, Get Ahead, Leeds.

The three key lessons that can be taken from this book are these:

1. Identify your purpose

It's important to find your purpose by really being honest with yourself to understand what your motivators are for working, both monetary and non-monetary. If there is one thing I want you to take away, it's to challenge the traditional ways of working, and to recognise that professional and credible work can be achieved in a non-traditional and much more flexible way. I want you to appreciate that there are other ways of working than slogging your guts out in a traditional nine-to-five role, never seeing your children and never feeling good enough.

2. Maintaining a positive growth mindset

It's critical to have the correct mindset when running your own business, so you need to be honest with yourself and understand how to maintain a positive growth mindset that will set you on the right course. It's vital to develop and maintain a positive attitude when running your own business, which you can apply to all aspects of your business to help you succeed.

3. Take the correct action

Everything relies on the correct action and the ability to actually make things happen. Without consistent action, nothing will happen! Remember our tips for helping you keep on track: having a designated working space, dressing appropriately and working to a bespoke timetable every day. Writing and actioning a to-do list really helps you focus, and having daily rituals keeps you on track. Communicating effectively can work wonders, as does taking breaks and getting out from behind your desk.

I'm ready to support you in making the best decision of your working life. Our franchise opportunity will give you the flexibility and balance that you're craving. The fact that this is a scalable business model means that it can grow with you. You won't regret it, I promise!

Come and join our growing Get Ahead family; your journey to opportunity is waiting to start, so get in touch today!

What's Next?

If you've come to end of this book and feel that you would like to learn more, please get in touch with us today!

Call us on 01483 332220 or email office@getaheadva.com

We can't wait to hear from you so that we can talk about how you could become our next Get Ahead regional director!

References

Asefesco, A. (2015). *Franchise Business: A powerful winning strategy for business growth in any economy.* AA Global Sourcing. https://tablo.io/ade-asefeso/franchise-business-a-powerful-winning-strategy

Bolles, R.N (2019). *What colour is your parachute?* Ten Speed Press.

Branden, N. (1995). *Six pillars of self-esteem.* Random House.

British Franchise Association (2018). *BFA Natwest franchise survey 2018.* https://thebfa.microsoftcrmportals.com/shop/bfanatwest-franchise-survey-2018/

Chartered Institute of Personnel and Development (2019). *UK working lives.* https://www.cipd.co.uk/Images/uk-working-lives-2019-v1_tcm18-58585.pdf

Dweck, C. (2007). *Mindset: The new psychology of success: How we can learn to fulfil our potential.* Ballantine Books.

FreeAgent (2019). *2.6 Million Brits aim to become their own boss in 2019, research reveals.* https://www.freeagent.com/company/press-room/millions-of-brits-aim-to-become-own-boss/

Gough, O. (2017). *Self-employed earn more and work less than salaried workers.* Small Business. https://smallbusiness.co.uk/self-employed-salaried-workers-2536479/

Hall, J. (2018). *Self-employed are the happiest workers.* Simply Business. https://www.simplybusiness.co.uk/knowledge/articles/2018/04/self-employed-are-the-happiest-workers/

HM Treasury (2019). *Rose review of female entrepreneurship.* https://assets.publishing.service.gov.uk/government/uploads/system/uploads/attachment_data/file/784324/RoseReview_Digital_FINAL.PDF.

Keller, J. (2012). *Attitude is everything.* Pentagon.

Key performance indicator (n.d.) In *Lexico.com.* https://www.lexico.com/definition/key_performance_indicator

Minor, K. (2020). *Kory Minor training and consulting.* https://www.koryminortraining.com/

Mumpreneur (n.d.). In *Collinsdictionary.com.* https://www.collinsdictionary.com/dictionary/english/mumpreneur

Myers, C. (2018). *How to find your ikigai and transform your outlook on life and business.* Forbes. https://www.forbes.com/sites/chrismyers/2018/02/23/how-to-find-your-ikigai-and-transform-your-outlook-on-life-and-business/#47c787c2ed44

Office for National Statistics (2018). *Business demography, UK: 2018.* https://www.ons.gov.uk/businessindustryandtrade/business/activitysizeandlocation/bulletins/businessdemography/2018#:~:text=The%20survival%20rates%20show%20the,42.4%25%20(Figure%202).

Office for National Statistics (2019). *Employment and employee types.* https://www.ons.gov.uk/employmentandlabourmarket/peopleinwork/employmentandemployeetypes

Prowess (n.d.). *Facts about women in business.* https://www.prowess.org.uk/facts/

Royal Society for Public Health (2016) *Health in a hurry: The impact of rush hour commuting on our health and wellbeing.* https://www.rsph.org.uk/our-work/policy/wellbeing/commuter-health.html

Vitality Health (2017). *Long commutes costing firms a week's worth of staff productivity.* https://www.vitality.co.uk/media/long-commutes-costing-a-weeks-worth-of-productivity/

Work-life balance (n.d.). In *Lexico.com.* https://www.lexico.com/definition/work-life_balance

Further Reading

Bolles, R.N (2019). *What colour is your parachute?* Ten Speed Press.

Branden, N. (1995) *Six pillars of self-esteem.* Random House.

Dweck, C. (2007). *Mindset: The new psychology of success: How we can learn to fulfil our potential.* Ballantine Books.

HM Treasury (2019). *Rose review of female entrepreneurship.* https://assets.publishing. service.gov.uk/government/uploads/system/uploads/attachment_data/ file/784324/RoseReview_Digital_FINAL.PDF

Keller, J. (2012). *Attitude is everything.* Pentagon.

Royal Society for Public Health (2016) *Health in a hurry: The impact of rush hour commuting on our health and wellbeing.* https://www.rsph.org.uk/our-work/policy/ wellbeing/commuter-health.html

Acknowledgements

Writing a book has always been a dream of mine, so I want to give a huge thank you to the wonderful Lara Doherty from The Motivation Clinic for spurring me into action after I attended her vision-board class and a book appeared on my board! This led me to gain confidence and start my book-writing journey, and I reached out to Alexa Whitten, a book coach I was recommended. I'm a huge advocate of coaching, having worked with a variety of business coaches ever since setting up Get Ahead. I respond well to working one to one with someone, so it made perfect sense to do this with my book project too. And it worked like a dream! Alexa kept me on the straight and narrow, she helped draw my book out of me, and she gave me the clarity and confidence to keep going. For this, I'll be forever grateful.

Talking of coaches, I have to thank my business coach Nell Op de Beeck for her constant positivity and encouragement when it comes to anything I do, and my book writing was no exception! Nell put up with my book writing appearing in all my 90-day plans for what felt like months, and she was forever boosting me if I felt discouraged. Thanks Nell – you're simply the best and one of my top cheerleaders.

Franchising as an option for scaling my business was introduced to me by the franchise king himself, Berkeley Harris! I had listened to Berkeley speak at a conference, we met face to face subsequently, and working with him enabled me to scope out an appropriate way to franchise the business and to give other people an amazing opportunity to carve out a flexible way to work. Thanks for your continued support, Berkeley – it means a lot.

I want to give a special mention to Carrie Jones who piloted the franchise for me in 2017. Carrie was the answer to my prayers; we learnt so much together, and I couldn't have chosen a better partner in crime!

Without my team at Get Ahead, there would be no book, so this is a special mention to all my franchisees around the UK and to my growing team of VAs – you're my professional family, and I'm beyond delighted at all that we've achieved collectively since I launched the business in 2010. With the current pandemic, we've become even closer, playing – in the words of my franchisee Marie Peters – "the long game". We're non-competitive and super caring about all members of the team, and I couldn't be prouder of you all. My designers Kate and Shea have helped bring this book content alive, and I can't thank you both enough – you're both so patient and have the knack of interpreting my rather garbled briefs immediately!

Our clients are clearly the fuel for our business, and, again, the business wouldn't be here without their loyalty and trust in us. I want to say a special thank you to our client Desiree Anderson, who was incredibly helpful when I was stuck for a book title; *Virtually Yours* was her input, and I loved it immediately!

My parents set up a tutorial agency in 1970, which my mother ran throughout my childhood, and I really feel that this gave me the encouragement and motivation to run my own business. Not everyone has the entrepreneurial drive needed to run and develop a sustainable business, so I want to thank my parents for allowing me to witness this first-hand from such a young age.

My final acknowledgement goes to my husband Martin and our daughters – Issy, Aimee and Robyn. I think you'll all be relieved now that this book is written and published; it will no longer be used as a reason why I can't do something! Thanks for your patience and encouragement. I owe you all so much, but hope that you can now understand why I needed to get this book out of my head and onto paper.

About Rebecca and Her Team

Rebecca Newenham founded Get Ahead in 2010. After seven years of successfully growing her award-winning virtual agency, she welcomed her first franchisee in 2017. Since then, she's gone on to add franchisees from Wakefield in the north right down to Woking in the south. As a virtual agency, Get Ahead helps businesses of all sizes and from all sectors to get ahead.

Rebecca grew up knowing that she wanted to run her own business one day, just like her mother did. After university, Rebecca enjoyed a career in corporate buying in London, working for retail giants Superdrug and Sainsbury's. She loved the fast pace of retail, but once her daughters had been born, she decided to take a step away from the career ladder. When her youngest started school, the time felt right to start her own business.

Being able to work flexibly around her family was key. After researching various options and seeing how the economic landscape was shaping up after the 2008/9 recession, Rebecca decided to launch a virtual agency. Though the term 'virtual assistant' was relatively unknown in the UK back then, it was well established in the United States, and she could see the potential. Outsourcing enables agile businesses to keep fixed costs low and to respond quickly to market changes.

By 2016, the business had seen years of sustained revenue growth. The team and the range of business services they offered had expanded, as had their client base. They had even won a 'Flexible Business of the Year' award. However, Rebecca was keen to take the business to the next level and unlock new growth opportunities.

Rebecca worked closely with a franchise consultant and took the time to develop the right franchise offering. In 2017, she welcomed her first franchisee on board, and it has been an exciting journey ever since. Mentoring and supporting her franchisees is so rewarding. Rebecca talks about going into business for yourself but not by yourself, as she's there to support her franchisees every step of the way.